Honorable Harvey Pitt Former Chairman, Securities and Exchange Commission – "Phil Johnston's book is a valuable resource for any entrepreneur, and fills a definite need."

General Hugh Shelton, former Chairman of the Joint Chiefs of Staff – "Phil Johnston provides a superb guide to leading and managing a small business and does it with a great sense of humor. A thoroughly enjoyable 'must read'!"

Mr. Erskine Bowles, President of the Consolidated University of North Carolina – "Everyone included in small business needs a sense of humor just to survive. *Success in Small Business Is a Laughing Matter* captures the essence of small business and its joy like few others."

Dr. Nido R. Qubein, President of High Point University – "You'll love this book for its insights and its wisdom and you'll find yourself reflecting on its content often. I highly recommend it."

Congressman Howard Coble, North Carolina – "The small business community is the engine that generates American commerce. This is a must handbook for the large numbers of newly minted entrepreneurs starting their own businesses, especially the unprecedented number of women signing up to be entrepreneurs in America."

SUCCESS IN SMALL BUSINESS IS A LAUGHING MATTER

By
J. Phillips L. Johnston, J.D.

"The best book ever written about small business"

~ Esquire ~

Bloomington, IN Milton Keynes, UK

authorHOUSE™

AuthorHouse™
1663 Liberty Drive, Suite 200
Bloomington, IN 47403
www.authorhouse.com
Phone: 1-800-839-8640

AuthorHouse™ UK Ltd.
500 Avebury Boulevard
Central Milton Keynes, MK9 2BE
www.authorhouse.co.uk
Phone: 08001974150

First published by AuthorHouse 6/29/2007

ISBN: 1-4184-4667-X (sc)
ISBN: 1-4184-4666-1 (dj)
ISBN: 1-4184-6593-3 (e)

Printed in the United States of America
Bloomington, Indiana

This book is printed on acid-free paper.

Being a founder is special whether founding a nation, an organization, or an important discovery. In business, founder is a title of respect, outranking chairman or chief executive officer. Dr. Eugene Grace, M.D., is the founder of this book. But for his vision, this book would still be ephemeral. Many regret, along with me, that Dr. Grace closed Moore Publishing Company when he took his sabbatical to China after publishing Success in Small Business is a Laughing Matter.

This fourth edition is published by AuthorHouse, a publisher on demand (POD).

Dedication

To my wife, Dottie, and my children, Jamie, Shannon, Phillips, and Nick, who have added so much joy to my life.

Table of Contents

Ode To Curiosity

Charlotte Liebig has proven to be an editor extraordinaire and a soul mate. Curiosity is the first requisite to edit a humorous book about entrepreneurship. It might well be the first requisite for a fulfilled life. To satisfy her almost unquenchable thirst to lap knowledge at the oracle of Delphi, she reads encyclopedias as regular fare. Even Winston Churchill, who read most major dailies every morning in bed, is not reported to be a reader of encyclopedias, even Volume Q, likely the most intriguing by virtue of its small size and oddball letter. How much subject matter of interest has that misfit Q as its introduction? Curious minds like Charlotte's seek an answer to that question.

Yes, it doesn't hurt that she passed the New York BAR, the Gold Standard. It doesn't hurt that she is unabashedly "geekish" when it comes to understanding our wired age. These things, coupled with her curiosity, make her an inveterate researcher, a quality which has had a direct impact upon the quality and breadth of this book.

But, best of all, she has an inquisitiveness to not only know, but to know why. Love disappears. Wealth is fleeting. Desire cools. But curiosity, in its purest state, settles in the soul forever. A friend, colleague and helpmate in every sense, Charlotte is the most curious person I've ever had the pleasure of knowing.

Foreword

With such a plethora of do-it-yourself "entrepreneurship" books hitting the market lately, I approached Phil Johnston's new literary venture in this area with appropriate skepticism. Two hours later, after I had stopped laughing from my encounter with the "Tax-Free Cat Ranch", I was convinced that Phil had indeed come up with something really new, appropriately specific, unbelievably funny in the right places, and, on balance, of significant help to the budding entrepreneur.

As the instructor of the University's only entrepreneurship course, I have long wished for a book which would present a working balance between the "institutional" issues in entrepreneurship (such things as form of organization, tax laws, organization structure, bank borrowing, employee compensation, etc.) and the more gutsy personal issues which inevitably seem to make the difference between success and failure in new ventures (things like personality, ambition, bargaining skills, sense of timing, boredom-aversion needs, and need to escape the "rat race"). Phil's book, *Success in Small Business Is a Laughing Matter,* does well by the reader when it comes to discussing the tax advantages of a Subchapter S corporation, presenting your need for capital to the banking community successfully and providing a useful orientation to new employees. However, it also deserves kudos for facing up to "how to choose a CPA," deciding whether "You can stand to have a control over your own destiny," and "finding out whether you have the humility to be effective." Phil Johnston has some sage advice on each of these issues and on many more in this cleverly written and arranged book. He writes with the assurance of someone who has "done it" successfully and the fact that he has done just that becomes apparent to the reader early and with lasting impact. The tone is light but persuasive, the informational content is laudable, the frankness is genuinely appreciated, and the cartoons are short of fantastic. To anyone even remotely contemplating starting up his/her own little venture, I say read Phil Johnston on the subject. You will be entertained, informed, and helped far beyond the cost of this volume.

Richard Levin
Professor of Business Administration
University of North Carolina Chapel Hill, North Carolina

Executive Summary

Why should we want to be a small business owner? It is the great American dream. It insures job security inasmuch as you cannot fire yourself.

The independence and freedom of ownership as well as the satisfaction of seeing the direct results of your decisions are still more reasons to become an owner.

There will be a glut of managers in the first several decades of the 21st century. As a small business owner, you will avoid the rat race of the management group vying for jobs in large businesses.

The challenge of ownership is clearly a reason to become your own boss. The broad range of issues and challenges you will face will stimulate you and be vastly rewarding in the long run.

From an economic point of view, small business ownership allows you to build an estate in addition to earning a salary. Small business ownership allows you the same tax advantages available to top management of larger businesses. Consider also that the road the large corner office occupied by top management in the monoliths forms to the rear and usually takes a quarter-century to navigate. These are the major reasons why you should consider entrepreneurialism.

It is urged that extensive soul searching be done before becoming a small business owner. Make sure your motive is to become an entrepreneur, not to run away from an unhappy situation. Also, be sure you are not like the suicidal who carve out careers with the goal of self-destruction. Captain Ahab lives!

It is also imperative that you take a careful inventory of your management skills to ascertain that you have the combination of grit, education and applied management skills developed during a five-year (more or less) management internship with a large company. You will know the best time to leave the training ground provided by your manager/mentor. In this volume, we call him Mr. Goolsby, a hapless, less-than-loveable CEO of a large company. Remember though, if you don't sail until all dangers are past, you will never leave port.

You also must be able to embrace the different lifestyles required of certain small businesses, especially the long hours demanded of new owners.

Avoid starting your own business from the ground up. Unless you have an iron will, don't require sleep, and have an excess of cash in reserve to throw at research and development, it is preferable to invest in a "going concern" where you will enjoy the comfort of an existing trade name, and standardized product or service line. In your plan, which you will want to commit to writing, include the criteria you are looking for in your search for a going business to purchase. You should also include in your written master plan economic scenarios which you believe will unfold in the future. Predictions are useless. Scenario planning is useful. This will help you to purchase a business which can take advantage of expected growth in a particular area, such as nanotechnology, a science of manipulating matter at the atomic level to build microscopic devices and materials molecule by molecule. The National Science Foundation estimates the market for nanotechnology products and services will reach $1 trillion (the wonderful "T" word) dollars by 2015 in the United States alone. Nanotechnology appears to embody Joseph Schumpeter's coined term "creative destruction:" how unexpected innovations destroy markets and give rise to new fortunes. You want your new venture to destroy and replace the old technology,

Most underestimate the need for money--hard cash. Go against the grain by acquiring a business which is losing money because of inept management or because of the heavy start-up expenses of a new business founded by others. Consider assuming some of the company's debts. Much less money will be needed in that case.

You still will need money to operate your business. Small businesses have a seemingly insatiable appetite for money, usually for working capital to support expanding sales. A direct loan from the Small Business Administration is your best source. The interest rate is so low relative to alternative sources that I encourage you to borrow up to the statutory maximum and worry about what to do with the money later. Few of these loans are granted, however, because of limited federal funding for this program. At this point, your versatile commercial banker becomes your best money source (and friend!). Even though banks have a number of better places to invest money than in a small business, you can still get the loan if you develop the loan officer's friendship and smother the banker with a mass of figures, statistics, projections and analyses of your business. If you run into the rare situation of a bank with a qualified in-house financial analyst who understands this mass of figures, quickly change banks.

Lastly, apply for a commercial bank loan guaranteed by the Small Business Administration (SBA). These SBA guaranteed loans are sweet deals for the banks because they get to charge the market interest rate even though up to 90% of the bank loan is backed by your federal government. Your company will have excellent potential because it fits into all or most of the criteria they have established and is part of a potential growth market. By taking over a failed business, you will replace inept management—you know, the guy who swallowed the goldfish.

What do we do after we have acquired a going concern? How do we successfully function as a small business owner? Why is it that some entrepreneurs succeed while others fail? The successful owners spew profits out of their companies while the failures could not make a bigger mess if they had taken a rotten avocado and dashed it against the pavement.

Let's look at a number of characteristics and attributes of the successful *numero uno*. Certain people make things work in an ethical way. They always come out on top one way or the other. These people exercise leadership by example. They live the sermon. They know that employees emulate deeds and actions. Words not backed up and committed by one's actions are hollow, signifying nothing. Accordingly, stoicism, ethics, humility and a genuine concern for all employees is practiced by the owner who sets the example.

Organization is frequently buried beneath mission in the entrepreneur's mind. Accordingly, heavy emphasis should be placed on organization as your small business prospers and grows. A Quick Read™ organizational chart with a brief job description of each management slot has been conceived and introduced by the author especially for small business (See Chapter 10). The chart shows where each manager fits into the company and what, in brief, the manager does. The chart is useful in understanding and planning the corporate structure. The selection and promotion of managers in this chart is critical. The importance of hourly employees with their strong work ethic (needing only leadership) is greatly stressed. Motivation of all people in the company is essential to your success. Even though not embraced by corporate America, it is essential that all employees fully understand and believe in the benefits your product or service provides others. We all genuinely want to serve others and to benefit humankind. With the Industrial Revolution prostrate on history's gurney, the new knowledge worker in this Age of Ideas asks: "Has humanity been well served?" The question, "Did we achieve our goals and expected bottom line?" comes later.

Various methods of communicating effectively both within the company and outside the company are explored, with inexpensive audiovisuals getting the nod as the best communications method in most situations.

The dress of the business world for merit is the conservative dark suit, white shirt, plain black socks and traditional dark lace-up wingtips. Subdued stockings and dark shoes for woman with the same dark suit and white silk blouse are preferred. Lose the polyester, argyle socks, Disney ties and white sport coats with pink carnations. Thou shall not dress flashy now that thou art a successful owner. If you business requires less formality, always present a neat, tailored and clean appearance.

Select outside professional people based solely on experience and ability. Count the crows-feet around their eyes. This is a guaranteed sign of experience…or insomnia.

The giant web of government regulations and government harassment is far and away the biggest threat to the small business sector, and, unless corrected by the strong and resolute among us, could make small business go the way of the woolly mammoths.

The ability to digest information and current events in our fast-changing, internet world is essential to successful decision making. Being able to understand information about your own company through financial statements is essential. The balance sheet is the most important financial statement followed by the cash flow statement. The profit and loss statement is a distant third.

Marketing is the infantryman of small business.

Finally, for every front-line dogface, ten support soldiers are needed for this infantryman. Even if all ten in support are military whizzes, the battle will still be lost if but one infantryman is a dud. Accordingly, the production and financial functions should not be given co-equal status with marketing but should be treated as an extension of marketing. Marketing is the locomotive that pulls small business forward. Knowing small companies cannot compete with the substantially lower unit costs of the larger companies which dominate the market in that particular product, smalls must *create* a protected market niche in order to compete effectively with the behemoths. Your single goal as a small business owner is to have dominant market share in that niche.

An entrepreneurial focus coupled with imagination and creativity has been and will always be our nation's sustainable competitive advantage. Let your fulcrum – starting right now – be entreprenship coupled with hope. Think what to do next, not who to blame next.

As a newly-minted entrepreneur, you are part of your nation's number one export – Yankee ingenuity and creativity. The world has always looked our way for that kind of leadership and vision. Be bold! Be Brave! Stake your claim to the heritage that has made our nation a superpower and the envy of the world.

Now go forth, Braveheart. You will be amply rewarded. You will be happier. You will make the world a better place for all of us.

Chapter 1
Why Become a Small Business Owner?

Will You Sign In, Please?

G. A. Goolsby

Many of us observe with sadness our friends who trudge through life in management positions with big companies. Completely devoted, they risk coronary infarctions to earn gold watches upon retirement, which is usually followed by severe cases of amnesia among co-workers who tend to remember them as "Jonathan who"? This is their reward for spending their lives under the risk of being fired at any moment as they struggle to climb the corporate ladder.

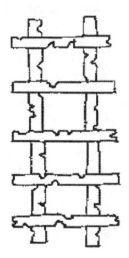

Executive ladder with extensive termite damage.

One morning as you pick up the Sunday paper the startling truth hits: You and I are the management acquaintances we have been observing. We are in bondage to our corporate monolith, and Mr. Goolsby, the bloodless chairman of the board (sometimes called the smiling cobra), has us in an uneasy quest for job recognition.

Goolsby is a stereotype of the big company chieftain. The slab of fat on his chin hangs loosely like a rooster's crop and jiggles like jelly when he moves. The old-timey pleats in his trousers puff out to make him look as if he had swallowed a melon, and he constantly twiddles a used string in nervous frustration.

His office decor is a tribute to Louis XIV: a cross between Versailles and a French bordello. A faint odor of pluff mud is ever present. You almost wonder if his bulging goldfish eyes are a result of his intense ambition or hunger. Goolsby is a humorless old fogey, but the main complaint, especially by the junior executives, is that the *boss does not practice the type of management he preaches.*

When he doesn't know the answer to a question, Goolsby mumbles down his sleeve rather than utter the executive's hardest concession: "I don't know."

His two rules for success by underlings are straightforward: Rule 1. The boss is always right. Rule 2. In any other situation refer to Rule 1.

Mr. Goolsby

A so-so lover in his prime, which has long since passed.

Mr. Goolsby insists on many meetings, perhaps the greatest productivity killer on the planet. This is a result of management philosophies that value consensus at considerable expense to productivity growth; the cost substantially exceeds the benefit. The meetings establish two facts: first, Mr. Goolsby is, in fact, the boss, and, second, some of his subordinates are good guessers at what he likes to hear them say.

Even his "trophy" wife holds him in contempt. She's not alone. Sometimes you just want to wring his fat, frog-like neck.

As If Goolsby Wasn't Enough...

People fall prey to what Irving Janis called "group think." They become increasingly sure of the infallibility of their collective judgment. They listen mainly to each other and stress the need for consensus. They don't think to ask the hard questions, behaving instead as if there were no hard questions worth contemplating. Alfred Sloan, the father of modern day GM, said at the end of a meeting, "Gentlemen, I take it that we are all in complete agreement on the decision here. Then, I propose that we postpone further discussion…to give ourselves time to develop disagreement and perhaps gain some understanding of what the decision is all about." Sloan, wisely, recognized that dissent does not mean dissension. Debate facilitates quality decisions.

President Kennedy was said to have been an excellent thinker, and his brain trust was said to have been the best group of presidential advisors ever. But some people believe the Bay of Pigs decision was made in a large committee meeting when the brain trust gave opinions it thought the Commander-in-Chief wanted to hear, rather than what they really believed about invading Cuba. Can you imagine how else this poor decision was made by such a brilliant group of people? Unfortunately for the country, the brain trust must have been working within the framework of a typical business meeting, which usually does not involve much thinking but is, rather, a game of trying to say what the senior member wants most to hear.

The crunch of competition among young business men and women anxious to join the ranks of higher management has grown much worse in our lifetime, owing primarily to the baby boom of the late Forties and so many more job seekers with college degrees. Because of the low birth rates before and after, this group of war babies is like a melon being digested by a boa constrictor. And these cohorts have ripened into working adults.

In the decade spanning 1975-85, the number of 30- to 40-year olds in the U.S. population increased by 12 million, a record jump of 45 % over the previous decade. What impact will this have on the executive work force in the future? Using the usual 10% rule of thumb to determine how many will reach the level of corporate management, there were 1.2 million more 49- to 59-year olds in the executive ranks by 2004.

During most of the past 25 years, management talent has been in great demand with employers bidding up pay and fringe-benefit packages and considerable hard work by recruiters. But, no more.

Stephen Dresch, president of the Institute for Demographic and Economic Studies in New Haven, Conn., warns of "persistent saturation of the highly educated labor market" over the next 30 years. "In a traumatic reversal of historical experience," he says, "children born to parents who entered adulthood in the 1950s and 1960s will, on average, experience relatively lower status than their parents." This will reflect both declining educational attainments, induced by the saturation of the highly educated labor market, and the appropriation of career opportunities facing those who do in fact complete education programs.

Because of the shortage of 45- to 60-year olds (from which managers are usually drawn), it would seem that this abundance of young managers has arrived just in time and will soon be absorbed into top management. However, top management ability is achieved through experience and seasoning. It is earned and not declared, as the youthful managers of the go-go equity funds of the 1990s learned. In short, the skills and abilities of top management are not possessed by these young, newly arrived managers, and an edict by the king cannot make it otherwise. In fact, any King who would make such an edict has no more business savvy than the clueless monarch in the comic strip "The Wizard of Id."

Further crowding the ranks, an increasing number of women and minority group members seeking management positions have significantly contributed to the growing supply of management candidates, and, in turn, has heightened competition.

Working women have added substantially to the labor supply, with the ratio of workingwomen to working men approaching almost even. Eli Ginzberg, chairman of the National Commission on Manpower Policy, describes the revolution in the roles of women as "the single most outstanding phenomenon of the century," one that "will have a greater impact than the rise of communism and the development of nuclear energy."

Even the expected healthy level of demand for management talent will not take up this over-supply of management caliber people until well into the late 2010s, if then.

By economic law, the prices for management people will remain depressed, and competition will continue to be keen, even savage, during future business downturns. John Peterson, director of executive programs at the University of Southern California, as reported in *Duns,* believes that the competition for jobs could become so ferocious that a black market could develop with young managers bidding for the available jobs and offering bribes to personnel and other management people. Some even believe there could be demonstrations by young management people all over the country. Although these are clearly minority views, they underline the message. Ironically, those who hold jobs with large companies with limited futures will tend to cling to the security of the large companies rather than tasting the honey of small business living. This will aggravate further the shortage of competent small business owner/managers.

The *Wall Street Journal* has reported that intense competition has already begun, particularly in the younger management ranks. The article gives examples of companies having frank, Dutch-uncle conversations with rising managers about the management glut and advising even some of the more promising among them that opportunities and promotions might be less likely to come their way very quickly.

In addition to lowering executives' expectations, companies are giving lateral transfers to keep the managers' interest up, with fewer promotions being available. The granting of extra titles, aptly called "title inflation," is widely used to "stroke" managers. The management bottleneck has caused some companies to give the title of "president" in lieu of "plant manager" of small subsidiaries, for example. Not only are their egos bolstered, but the newly titled "presidents" have higher identification in their communities, and their sense of corporate responsibility is reinforced.

Sen. Daniel Patrick Moynihan, commenting on the importance of population shifts, once mused that "the great decisions of the world are made by solitary couples - male and female - and are made in bed to boot", about the only humor to be added to the management glut just over the horizon.

Even more significant than the executive surplus is that there are three other and very important reasons why men and women standing (perhaps shakily) on the corporate ladder should think to abandon big business. Having taken advantage of the excellent management training available at most big business staff-level offices, and having decided to become a small business owner, the candidates will know that:

1. They can better control their own destinies.
2. They can see the results of their work.
3. They can build estates in addition to earning salaries.

As Oscar Wilde said, "I used to think that money was the important thing in life. Now that I am old, I know it is."

Small business owners will think of other reasons for changing the pronoun "we" to the singular. Now, for example, they will be able to see the tangible results wrought by their decisions. Now they too will enjoy new freedom and independence; no longer will they have to spend two hours in a committee meeting making a decision which, in reality, should have been a matter of reflex. Add to all this the community esteem they will enjoy, as well as a type of job security not to be found in the ranks of corporate management, where fifteen or twenty years of solid service can sometimes earn you nothing more than a summary dismissal.

In short, the small business entrepreneur can never be axed!

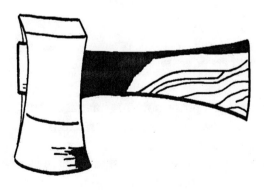

There are still other reasons to split from Mr. Goolsby's fiefdom. Small business ownership is extremely challenging and rewarding. The *Book of Lists* by Wallace, Wallace and Wallechinsky rates 23 typical jobs according to boredom:

		Boredom Rating
1.	Assembler (work paced by machine)	207
2.	Relief worker on assembly line	175
3.	Forklift-truck driver	170
4.	Machine tender	169
5.	Assembler (working at own pace)	160
6.	Monitor of continuous flow goods	122
7.	Accountant	107
8.	Engineer	100
9.	Tool and die maker	96
10.	Computer programmer	96
11.	Electrical technician	87
12.	Delivery service courier	85
13.	Blue-collar supervisor	85
14.	White-collar supervisor	72
15.	Scientist	66
16.	Administrator	66
17.	Train dispatcher	64
18.	Policeman	63
19.	Air traffic controller (large airport)	59
20.	Air traffic controller (small airport)	52
21.	Professor with administrative duties	51
22.	Professor	49
23.	Physician	48

* Reprinted from Tile Book of Lists by David Wallecllinsky, Irving Wallace, and Amy Wallace (Bantam Books, New York, 1977).
** Lawyers not listed. The authors did not consider the practice of law "honest" work.

Norman Martin, professor of management at New York University asserts, "Small business ownership is more challenging than many other careers, such as medicine or law."

It would necessarily follow that small business ownership would rank near the lowest according to boredom.

Chapter 2
Considerations Before Owning a Small Business

Before we march in on Mr. Goolsby and gleefully impale him, let us use the monolith's payroll to subsidize our transition from grunt to entrepreneur. Let's develop an overall objective.

Plan to spend about five years with a large company to develop and fine tune your management skills and about one-and-a-half years in the selection of a business to purchase.

During your five or so years, do your assignments well (even if Goolsby will get all the credit). You should carefully study the company's annual report. You will want to attend the shareholder's meeting, both your company's and others when possible. Involve yourself in the work of other departments, especially in those dealing with sales and advertising. Audit strategy meetings of top management wherever and whenever possible. Marketing is the heart of entrepreneurship. This is what you are preparing for.

The marketing mission must be carried out by capable people. Accordingly, involve yourself in personnel almost to the point of being a nuisance. Read the employee handbook and personnel policy books carefully. Get job descriptions and tables of organization and study them and learn from them for your own future company. Search out and attend all company sponsored courses. Enroll in company paid schools. Observe those managers who are on a fast track to the top. Why are they slotted for high office while others are doomed to mediocrity? In doing your assignments well you will not only earn your keep but also develop the management skills necessary for success as an owner.

The process of planning is much more than eenie, meenie, minee, mo. So few of us use long-range planning in our personal lives. Even E. I. DuPont, the father of corporate planning, budgeting and forecasting, paid scant attention to personal planning. Strange, that one. Go figure. We do not use long-range planning for our personal portfolio; neither do we use it for personal expenditure planning, either current or capital; nor for estate planning. We don't even use it for family planning.

Nevertheless, a detailed master plan is *mandatory* before one decides to become the owner of a small business. If you have not mulled the plan over for more than 18 months and not considered what your second career will look like two decades from now, you have not planned enough. Even before a plan is hammered out, some soul searching as to your motives for going into small business and an inventory of your personal qualifications are useful.

Why are you making the plunge? Are you tired of the commuter train ride to Manhattan? Are you the proud owner of a 60-foot sailboat with no time to use it? Did you get caught up in picking a career after school on what you thought was expected of you rather than what was important to you? Maybe your ambition is simply to follow the sun? Are you really escaping an unhappy family life and you think a change in location can help? Are you seeking a change solely to leave what has become an unbearable relationship with your present boss? Have you always wanted to get out of the bowels of the city into the country? Or are you just tired of doing what you are doing?

A personal-qualification inventory can be as revealing as an examination of your likes and dislikes:

Do you really want to succeed in your own business? Do you have the essential management skills? Are you thoroughly trained for your second career? The big bonus of freedom sought by those switching to small business has a price - long hours. Can you log in weeks working more than the allotted seven days? ("24 day weeks", as they're called...) Week after week? This is commonplace among new entrepreneurs. Can you drop out of the Monday night poker club? Can you store your golf clubs in the attic for three years?

Success in an executive suite with the added safeguard of group decision-making is not necessarily an indication that you possess the entrepreneurial abilities needed in small business. Also, many of us do not have the highly transferable management skills of the "chief executive officer type," the generalist or financial manager. Additionally, you might need the nerves of a high-wire artist, the patience of a brood hen, the cunning of a fox, and the judgment of a field marshal to master small business ownership. Even without these attributes, a second career as a small business owner is a fine idea if you have common sense, fondness for freedom, and a winner's attitude. It also helps to have a bent for power and control over others and an ability to balance tenacity and tough-mindedness.

A college background will serve you well. Management skill developed while employed with a professionally managed company is almost a must. It is helpful also to have a preference for results rather than for doctrine.

The type of business you choose - whether a bank or beauty shop - is not as important as you might think. The principles of management transcend any industry. How naive is the oft-heard slur that Mr. Newly-Arrived is an insurance man and not a tire maker?

A successful owner of an exploratory oil drilling company would be equally successful in an automotive parts business. On the other hand, a business hacker will, given enough responsibility and time, ruin any going concern - from machine manufacturing to massage parlor - regardless of how long he or she has been hanging around one industry.

There are certain likes and dislikes which deserve your consideration. You might consider in your master plan whether you can spend long hours and holidays at your company, if it is a retail business. The new owner of a bank had best enjoy hobnobbing with the wealthy. If you are entertaining the idea of a purchase of a manufacturer's representative organization, are you willing to spend days out of town with your sales people? You should certainly avoid a high technology industry if you find it unpleasant to deal with the typically independent-minded inventor/engineer type. Likewise, you should avoid purchasing a modeling agency if you are a womanizer.

I can resist anything but temptation

You certainly will want to avoid purchasing a capital intensive business dominated by larger companies. Vast capital can whip up on even the most inventive management mind. It's small

11

consolation that the lure of a business with a large capital-entry requirement may side-track some competition from small, low-capital businesses where your best employee will be competing with you tomorrow. Woe unto those who purchase a small business in an industry requiring large expenditures for research and development, especially if the new products have lengthy gestation periods. You've fallen into a painful trap! Unless you are a masochist, be cautious about starting your own business from scratch, particularly a manufacturing business.

Starting a franchise, of course, is not the same as starting your own business. With the former you start out holding a competitive edge. You enjoy, for example, the use of an existing trade name, as well as a distinctive business appearance and a standardized line of products and services. You also enjoy the advertising support of the parent organization, together with its marketing expertise. One can lift a franchise almost intact from the drawing board. Not so with a new business.

There are too many uncontrollable factors in starting a business. The unexpected is the norm. The accounting profession tries to bypass this with the capitalization and future-years write-off "organization expense," but the huge start-up expenses can never be properly measured by the bean-counters.

Consider, for example, the starting furniture manufacturer who makes a perfect prototype in his basement. As he produces his first suite, it comes to pass that the humidity of the mill has not been properly adjusted. The entire suite warps and suddenly *$60,000* worth of warped, finished furniture parts has to be sold at salvage.

The new small business owner must figure on being in the red for at least four years or possibly more. Examples are plentiful of the new-born small business owner who errs in planning for this period of loss. Those who are money sources for the venture, whether relatives or a commercial bank or even small business investment corporations, cannot grasp the phenomenon of start-up losses, and their initial enthusiasm may be supplanted by stage four of any major project even before the new small business can become profitable. *Search for the guilty!*

Stages of a Major Project

1. Enthusiasm
2. Disenchantment
3. Panic
4. Search for the Guilty
5. Punishment of the Innocent
6. Decoration for All Those Who Took No Part

. . . Anonymous

Your best chance of eliminating errors is on the drawing board in a *new* real estate project, but even in real estate a going project is preferred, particularly since recent legislation affords the same depreciation deduction (based on a fifteen year useful life) to new and used real property.

There are too many variables in starting a business and even venerable companies experience years of operating losses when starting a new company to sell to a captive market which, in many cases, is its parent company.

Once more, avoid *starting* your own business! At a minimum, if you must start, say, a consulting or business employment service, or similar type service business, at least set up the business part-time before switching over. There will be blood letting but maybe you can avoid hemorrhaging big red numbers.

You should, in your master plan, allocate time to observe those well-educated, disciplined managers who cut the umbilical cord to become owners rather than continue as technocrats of large companies. Still, the best source of information will be your present, sound-thinking business associates - not that they necessarily know so much about small business but mainly because they can help you isolate flaws as well as act as a sounding board to uncover fallacies yourself. Your family should be involved in your plans for a second career, if not for guidance, then for the preservation of domestic tranquility. The emancipated business owner, ironically, is a poor counselor in their quest for entrepreneurialism and will revel only in the emotional self-satisfaction of ownership and not ascertain the hard-core facts they will need in considering the transition they must make. They start out by telling you that there are only two types of people in the world: those who own a small business and those who want to own a small business. And from this premise all further syllogisms are formed. To cut this useless conversation short, you simply tell them that they are confused. The two types of people are, in reality, those who divide people into two types, and those who don't.

Fools might rush in, but you need not fear treading into the world of small business if you have a good, long-range plan and some old, common saw-file soul searching.

Chapter 3
Tax Advantages of Small Business Ownership

Small, privately owned corporations have significant tax advantages because small businesses have, for many years, been politically favored - much like the farmers - with legislation providing particular tax benefits. Even where the same tax laws apply, the privately held corporation has the advantage over a public corporation because personal tax planning inevitably influences company policy.

Tax advantages are great, and in small businesses, they are real enough to be actively pursued, but some guidelines should be considered:

1. Profits. The business must first be successful, producing either profits or positive cash flow; otherwise, tax planning is a vacuous exercise.

2. Professionals. Employ competent professionals, both legal and accounting, and make sure they are familiar with your business affairs on a continuing basis. Competent professionals are expensive but necessary to successful tax planning.

3. Be Involved. Understand each tax proposal. Consider its effect upon cash flow and employee morale as well as the tax savings involved. In addition, understand the basic legal principles involved; you will make the final decision on each tax proposal and will have to live with the result.

4. The Tax Tail. Do not allow the tax tail to wag the dog; most plans adopted purely for tax reasons end in disaster.

5. Tax Categories. Tax plans fall generally into two categories:

First are those which are guaranteed to produce the desired result if properly implemented. An example would be a decision to be taxed as an LLC, or Subchapter S or C corporation.

Second are those where the results depend upon subjective determinations or are uncertain for other reasons. For example, what amount constitutes a reasonable salary? Know which category you are dealing in, and if the results are uncertain, understand the consequences of an adverse result.

6. Take Chances. If you have employed competent professionals and understand the particular tax proposal, then do not hesitate to take chances. The large majority of tax planning is done in areas where results are not certain, and the timid frequently pay a high price for peace of mind.

7. Audits. If the Internal Revenue Service audits your business and proposes a significant tax deficiency, then consult with your tax lawyer who, at the least, can comfort you by telling you the difference between a tax collector and a taxidermist. The taxidermist leaves the hide. If he believes your case has merit, then do not hesitate to don your hobnailed boots and a dueling pistol and fight the government. In this area particularly, early concessions or settlements are frequently unnecessarily expensive.

8. Footnote. If the audit has raised the notion that your professionals may not be competent, then re-evaluate them. Perhaps you should cut them loose from their moorings and let them float out to sea. In most instances, your stomach will be a reliable guide, gut reactions being preferred to in-depth analysis. Remember though, if you have ventured into tax areas where results are not certain, audits and proposed tax deficiencies should be expected, and your lawyer's ability to resolve the matter on a basis which justifies the entire effort is the measure of his worth.

Some tax plans simply defer taxes. These plans have merit because the income may be deferred until a later year when your income tax bracket is lower, the funds otherwise used to pay taxes can be invested during the deferral period to produce additional income and at the end of the deferral period, the income taxes may be paid in less valuable dollars because of inflation and the time value of money. Qualified profit sharing and pension plans are typical tax deferral vehicles. Also, those selling their businesses for stock in the acquiring corporation or for promissory notes payable over several years can, in appropriate cases, utilize tax deferral techniques. Here's an example:

A friend and I plan to invest in a large cat ranch near Karmosille, Mexico. We would start rather small, with about one million cats. Each cat averages about twelve kittens a year; skins can be sold for about 20 cents for the white ones and up to 40 cents for the black.

This will give 12 million cat skins per year to sell at an average of around 32 cents, making our revenue about $3 million a year. This averages out to $10,000 a day - excluding Sundays and holidays.

A good Mexican cat man can skin about 50 cats a day at a daily wage of $3.15. It will take only 663 men to operate the ranch, so the net profit will be over $8,200 per day. Now, the cats will be fed on rats exclusively. Rats multiply four times as fast as cats. We will start a rat ranch right adjacent to our cat farm.

Here is where the first-year tax break really comes in. Since we will be utilizing the rats to feed the cats, we can expense the entire first batch of rats purchased just prior to the year end. If we start with one million rats, at a nickel each, we will have a whopping $50,000 tax deduction for the year even though the "cat rat food" will be used to generate income in the next year.

The rats will be fed on the carcasses of the cats we skin. This will give each rat one quarter of a cat per day. You can see by this that the business is a clean operation, self-supporting and really automatic throughout. The cats will eat the rats, and the rats will eat the cats, and we will get the skins and the tax benefits! Incidentally, our ecology consultants think it's great.

Eventually, we hope to cross the cats with snakes. Snakes skin themselves twice a year. This will save the labor cost of skinning and will also give us a yield of two skins for one cat. Viva el gato! (Note: No animals were harmed or abused in the preparation of this book. . .)

Other tax plans avoid payment of taxes permanently. In this category, consider the payments made by a corporation for medical expenses incurred by an officer, his wife or children. If a medical reimbursement plan is in effect for the corporation, it will deduct the payments and the officer (although the obvious recipient of an economic benefit) will not have taxable income. In this connection, it is important to note that most executives have high salaries, and that these taxpayers get little benefit from the personal deduction allowed for medical expenses. As a result, the officer avoids tax on the economic benefit received year after year by the corporation's payment of his medical expenses.

Tax plans also differ materially depending upon the industry or business involved. Obviously, farmers, doctors and manufacturers are faced with different tax planning opportunities. The shopping list of tax planning opportunities which appear below assumes a profitable, cash-healthy manufacturing corporation controlled by one or two stockholders who also serve as the corporation's chief executives. They seek to minimize income taxes for the company and themselves while at the same time withdrawing substantial funds from the corporation each year. The stockholders might consider:

1. *Fiscal year.* Each corporation may choose its fiscal year in its first income tax return. That is, the corporation may terminate its taxable year at any time during the first twelve months after organization, thereby creating a short taxable year. Because lower tax rates apply to the first $100,000 of corporate earnings each year, the short taxable year can afford two opportunities to use the lower rates during an eighteen month period. Likewise, if a Subchapter S corporation elects a January 31 fiscal year, taxation of its earnings to the stockholders will be postponed for one year (i.e., profits substantially earned by the corporation during 2006 will be taxed to its stockholders during their 2007 calendar year, and this one-year deferral continues indefinitely.)

2. *Salary.* The corporation can deduct reasonable compensation paid to its stockholder-employees. If the payments are unreasonably high, they will not be deductible but will be classified as dividends. This is a subjective area, but advantages can still be obtained, both in determining the amount and the timing of payments.

3. *Planes, Trains and Automobiles,* etc. Stockholder-employees frequently benefit from automobiles, memberships in city dining clubs, yachts, animal breeding ventures, airplanes, fishing and hunting retreats, and free medical checkups at resort-based clinics. However, caution should be exercised as these areas are subject to specific rules and reporting requirements, not infrequently involving litigation.

4. *Business Junkets, etc.* Business junkets are also quite legitimate. It's a fact that during the dead of winter, conventions and conferences in southern cities produce more valuable information

than do these meetings in northern cities. Likewise, when you're sweating buckets, business meetings in northern cities prove much more worthwhile than meetings south of the Mason-Dixon Line. Go figure! After all, it is not your fault that your supplier is domiciled in Lisbon, or that your industry's convention is being held at Miami Beach in the dead of winter or that the seminar on small business is to be in Palm Springs.

Confetti and hoorahs for business junkets

There are numerous opportunities in small corporations to minimize income tax consequences, such as retirement and medical reimbursement plans, stock options, ESOP's and other strategies to shift income and expenses. Also, substantial opportunities to defer or save income taxes are frequently available when businesses are bought or sold.

Many of these advantages are available to large businesses, but one typically has to be in top management, after waiting one's place in line (usually some twenty-five years long) before they can collect on them, assuming company policy allows such management perquisites.

Alas, if our present course holds true, it is leading to 100 % payroll withholding, and then none of us will have to bother with tax laws. Think of it. Your form 1040 would have only a blank for "gross wages and income" with only one instruction: send your check in amount equal to "gross wages and income". No accountants. No tax lawyers. No paperwork. No hassle. No money!

Chapter 4
Low Hanging and Ripe: Tax Benefits
For Venture Investments

It is common knowledge that over the long term *properly diversified* venture investments can yield higher returns than traditional S&P stock ownership. However, investors in small business and other venture investments should be reminded that the preferential tax treatment given to these types of investments can dramatically increase their effective yields. In order to create jobs and new business growth, the state and federal governments have enacted favorable tax treatments designed to promote direct investment in small businesses. The result is that you pay less tax on your venture investment gains.

Federal Incentives

1. Section 1244 stock allows the investor in a small C corporation ordinary losses rather than the usual capital losses up to $100,000 if married and filing a joint return.
2. Little-known Section 1045 of the Internal Revenue Code allows investors in C corporations to elect to defer any capital gains tax after selling qualified small business stock if the proceeds are reinvested in yet another qualified small business within 60 days.
3. Section 1202 provides that qualified small business stock in a C corporation held for more than five years qualifies for a 50 % gain exclusion on up to $10,000,000 or ten times the investor's base investment in the small business. The venture investor never has to pay tax on half of the investment gain! For example, Investor purchases stock in a qualified small business for $500,000. Five years and one day after the original purchase of the stock, Investor becomes eligible for the 50 % exclusion. If Investor sells the stock for $3,000,000, the gain is $2,500,000. Of this, she may exclude 50%, or $1,250,000, thus reducing the tax liability on the entire gain by one-half. Note that if the qualified small business gain dominates Investor's tax position, the alternative minimum tax may negate the benefits. Someone with significant ordinary income relative to the

size of the small business gain is the most likely to benefit from the incentive.

4. For all entities, here is another Federal incentive for entrepreneurs investing in venture companies: Section 83(b) allows a founder to receive *restricted stock* in a startup company as incentive compensation but pay ordinary income tax on the lower initial value of the founder's stock upon receipt. Later, appreciation and sale of the stock is taxed at the capital gains rate. Essentially, rather than pay the higher income tax rate on the value of the stock when it vests, the Section 83(b) election allows the founder to pay income tax only on the lower initial value of the restricted stock and pay at the capital gains rate on the appreciated value of the stock down the road.

State Incentives

Most commercial states have legislation to encourage new companies. North Carolina, for example, has created an incentive for small business investment regardless of business entity under Section 105-163 which allows an investor to claim up to 25 % of the amount invested as a *credit* against state income tax liability. An individual investor can claim up to $50,000 of tax credits against North Carolina income tax each year. Any unused credits can be carried over for five additional years. Investors can claim credits for investments made directly in Qualified Business Ventures or for investments made by pass-through entities such as S corporations, limited partnerships, and limited liability companies, if qualified. Some North Carolina investors have structured a $400,000 investment with the first installment invested in December and the $200,000 balance in January to earn a $100,000 credit.

Now that your eyes are crossed and your head hurts, alleviate your pain by speaking with your tax advisor about these tax treatments. Trust me, they enjoy this stuff! Selecting a good advisor or CPA is discussed in more depth in Chapter 20.

Chapter 5
Other Advantages of Small Business Ownership

Aside from tax advantages, owning your own business is an anti-inflation hedge, an often overlooked advantage of small business ownership. Since you are not dealing in a fixed income but rather in prices that can be adjusted regularly to pass on increasing costs, you can adjust to a bloated inflationary trend.

Another advantage of being a small business owner is that you can position yourself head-on against other small businesses which are often poorly managed. The lack of good management accounts for the shockingly high belly-up rate among small businesses. Dun & Bradstreet says that 90 % of all small business failures are caused by management deficiencies. It is submitted that this can be corrected by an increased level of college-trained people (and those trained in the art of management by large businesses) going into small business. On average, more than 1,000 small firms go out of business every day. Of the 500,000 new ownerships which develop annually, half do not last more than two years. Only 25 % survive as long as five years.

Typically, the management of the other small business - your competition - is third generation, and the present owner may well have his mind on a career on the concert stage denied him by Pop because the business needed him. Or, the owner, but for bearing the title of primogeniture, would be pumping gas and rearranging bugs on automobile windshields at the corner gas station. Or, he's the owner-son who returned home the first Halloween from Syracuse because of asthma aggravated by twenty degree below zero wind chills and regular four foot snowfalls. Or, he might be the son who works for the old S.O.B. (son-of-a-boss), and the interfamily rivalry is paramount to the profit and loss statement. He could be the prodigal tired of feeding at the corporate trough. He could be the fifty-year-old big business executive, recently dismissed for incompetence, who started a small business to piece back together his ego. Most likely, he is the failing owner who inherited the business from Pop but never had the opportunity to master the discipline of management. In that case, he would be the most prevalent and poignant of the small businessmen with whom you will compete. Although he wears many hats, as is required in all small businesses, he cannot even sport one that fits, like this little guy...

If all reasons grounded in logic - the tax benefits of a small business, building an estate, having "tenure" as owner, control of your own destiny and freedom, the satisfaction of seeing the results of your own work, the anti-inflation hedges available to a small business, the glut of management-grade people competing for few positions - fail to persuade you of the benefits of becoming a small business entrepreneur, then consider, as a last resort, an illogical reason to get out of the large business into your own venture: Everyone abhors big business!

Sit down and discuss with your teenage children (or anyone else's) their opinion of big business. According to a survey by Educational Communications, Inc. (assuming your teenager to be typical) he or she will immediately vituperate big business. They will tell you that large manufacturers are more interested in slick ads and pretty packages than the real facts or the quantity of the contents; big companies use their wealth to control the market, and are above the law. Conclusion? Those who run the largest corporations simply cannot be trusted. Witness Enron and Worldcom.

Incidentally, when questioned about factors influencing inflation, about one-third of the surveyed teenagers said that: (1) increased personal savings and investments contributed to inflation; (2) government efforts to reduce unemployment would curb inflation; (3) production of excess goods and services cause inflation.

It appears that our Mr. Goolsby is also the big business image of many American teenagers. The majority of American teenagers are clearly in error in their condemnation of large businesses (but on target about Goolsby). Moreover, their answer about the causes of inflation is the exact opposite of what is correct. Nevertheless, you can trust your teenager in giving you the correct guidance on what to do - go into your own small business - but for the wrong reason, namely, that big business is inherently bad.

Now, before impaling Mr. Goolsby on your corporate lance, and then breaking it off, let's get the benefit of management training available in big business and get on with your plan of becoming a small business owner.

**One Man's Pain
Is Another Man's Pleasure!**

Chapter 6
Selecting the Business to Purchase

What Is A Small Business?

When does a business cease to be small and become big? Are we talking big versus small in terms of people, assets, sales, net worth, profitability, margins, organizations or sales per employee?

By government definition, any company with assets below $9 million and earnings in the last two years of not more than $450,000 is classified as "small." This includes about 96 % of all businesses in the United States.

In my view, a small business is more broadly defined as one that is independently owned and operated and is not dominant in its field regardless of resources, earning power or number of employees. The emphasis is on freedom of action by the owner without outside interference and a market place that cannot be dominated by mere size alone.

Accordingly, Kaman Corporation of Bloomfield, Conn. (which purchased Currier Piano from me) is a small business even though the company has over $1 billion in sales and over $20 million EBITA with $400 million in total assets. Kaman is not dominant in either aerospace or musical instruments. It is easier to revise the definition of what constitutes a small business than it is to find a company that meets one's own criteria of what is desirable. One must realize at the outset that he or she is not likely to find the company which measures up to his or her ideal in every respect. It is a little like a man's search for the ideal woman. He dreams of a long-stemmed American rose: olive complexion, intelligent, blood-red narrow lips attached to a small mouth with tiny white teeth, and yet possessing an easy-going disposition and who is as carnal and sultry as Cleopatra. You awaken to realize that there is no way for this to happen considering your double hair lip, bald head polished and tight as the head of a snare drum, hairy little fingers, double belly roll and ogre's feet. You're never going to find exactly what you seek. Unlike Shrek, you'll not find your Princess Fiona.

Establishing Criteria

Even so you will be able to at least identify a risk to be weighed and assessed if you will rely on these suggested standards:

1. Choose to offer products or services which fit a continuing human need. Not a fad.
2. Any small company must have a specialized niche if it is to succeed - either a specialized product or a specialized service - or, failing either of those, a completely separate market where, because of geography or other factors, it may be a dominant force.
3. The business does not need expensive energy, advertising, legal advice, and the like. Keep your overhead low.
4. The business has as few employees as possible but high per capita sales.
5. Products that are difficult to copy or duplicate.
6. Low cash expenditures and cash revenues instead of credit, thereby keeping capital requirements to a minimum.
7. Choose a business relatively free of government harassment and regulations.
8. Choose a business which may be easily relocated if necessary.
9. Most of all, choose a business you can love.

Risk Considerations

The investment risk of small business ownership falls on the high end of the continuum. With such risks, why invest? Even though a small business has high risk, it also has the highest degree of payoff to the owner or owners.

Putting money into an insured savings account has little, if any, risk of loss, but, of course, the interest is modest at best. Bonds have higher returns, but you have more risk, including the risk of money market rates rising after purchasing the bonds. Gilt-edged common stocks, such as Procter & Gamble, have even more risks. Not only does the shareholder have an unsecured *last* claim on any remaining assets in the event of bankruptcy, a bad turn of company fortunes will send the share prices tumbling. The risk is undertaken because the shareholder owns the profits. If properly managed, profits abound, sending share prices soaring toward the North Star.

Tax shelters, such as exploratory oil drilling partnerships and leveraged real estate ventures, are even higher risks, but the return can be attractive to higher bracket investors. And then comes the small business ownership "cow's tail" with a risk so great it has been said that only the uninitiated rush in. You might do well to remember the old adage, "If it looks too good to be true, it probably is."

By analyzing what criteria to look for in a small business, by zeroing in on a growth market, by developing the necessary management skills and having the education, by leading with example, by being tough-minded and having guts and persistence, a great deal of the risk of small business ownership can be extracted. I know it can! With planning and preparation, the risk can be less, and the return greater than, owning publicly traded stock of a major blue-chip corporation.

Where Will Tomorrow's Growth Be?

The next step in selecting which business to buy is evaluating general beliefs concerning what tomorrow's business world might look like and which industry, or segment of an industry, might benefit.

We first want to lock into our thinking that the Industrial Revolution is prostrate on history's gurney. We witness today the Age of Ideas. The have-nots division is over knowledge, not money.

When an industry is in a growth cycle, even the less intelligent inhabiting boom city will make money. Conversely, an industry with the glide path of a stone (think textiles) can crush even the most nimble.

As we create scenarios, what we are addressing are future trends. These are not fads which fade rather quickly but mega-trends which will significantly shape our futures over the next ten to twenty years. We know one thing for sure about the future: it has already begun. If we scrutinize the present, we can trace the footprints in the sand and determine where they likely are going. Maybe Nostradamus, in all his prognosticating, needed only to see the obvious set before him!

Here are some scenarios we see developing. Remember that in all of these scenarios the Internet has become the marketing platform of choice:

27

1. **Fitness and Fitness Equipment.** Fitness and fitness equipment will grow increasingly popular, if not necessary. Exercise is becoming a part of our lifestyle, particularly among young adults. It aids weight reduction in our nation, where excess body weight has become a "full-blown" (pun intended) health crisis. Tennis, for example, will continue to boom. It requires little space. The cost of equipment and court time remain reasonable, and it is excellent exercise (though not as good as calisthenics). In a Gallup poll, tennis, along with softball or baseball, was named by teenaged females as their favorite sport. More importantly for the future of tennis, these girls picked tennis far-and-away as the sport they'd like to play but don't know how.

For the same reasons you can ditto handball, squash, jogging, racket ball, and bicycling. Hence, tennis and jogging shoes, cushion sole recreational socks, warm-up suits, racket strings and similar equipment will grow dramatically. Considering this, you can no doubt see ways to position yourself to take advantage of this expected growth, even if you purchase your own advertising firm by keying ad material off what would be our female teen's favorite sport if she could play tennis.

By these standards golf offers no exercise whatever, and the cost of land and construction, together with meeting the requirements of environmental regulations in constructing a course, would be prohibitive. The game is also too time-consuming. It takes years to reach a minimum level of proficiency. Hence, any golf-related industry should be avoided.

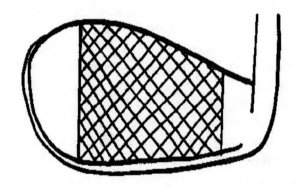

2. **Weight Control.** The "porking up" of America is the *biggest* mega-trend of our time. This phenomenon will open a Pandora's box of moneymaking opportunities for entrepreneurs with an *appetite* for cash. The *growth* will be so *off the scale*, even late adapters will make money.

Dr. Julie Gerberding, the Director of the Centers for Disease Control, has said that 65% of U.S. adults are either overweight or obese. The federal government's Weight-control Information Network ranks 65% of Americans over the age of 20 as overweight and sixty-one million Americans (31%) as obese, even as that population has tried to eat more healthfully.

There are many interesting "whys" for the fattening of America. Perhaps it's a reward for our ever-growing prosperity, but, our focus is how to make YOU prosperous.

One day, maybe not in my lifetime or yours, there will be a "fat pill" which will magically make all those pounds disappear without the work of diet and exercise. That would goose up an IPO bigger than Google! Meanwhile, there are a hundred ways to make money as the world indulges its gluttony: health/fitness franchising, health-oriented cookbooks, oversize clothing for the well-fed, new lines of clothing to wear while exercising ("leo-lards", anyone?), and the list goes on. Here's a stay-at-home CEO idea -- become a weight "consultant" and charge a monthly fee with a series of bonuses to be paid for pounds shed. You would have no investment other than your fitness knowledge (Simple -- It's the portions, Stupid...) and refer medical check-ups by contract. If you enjoy working with people and stay with it, you could grow a comfortable lifestyle company. Maybe you could name it Shaving Pounds? Ironically, recent studies have found that attitudes toward overweight people are shifting and becoming more accepting. Market research indicates that Americans who said they find overweight people "less attractive" dropped from 55% to 24%!

But, as long as the measure of a person's health is inability to fit into the airplane seat (always next to me!), there will be opportunities to spin all those excess calories into gold. I'm sure health care providers will be the first to invest.

3. **Alternative Fuel and Transportation.** Alternative fuel and battery operated vehicles will become the transportation of choice.

There are those who believe that electric cars will dot our nation's roadways, almost completely replacing the gas-guzzling, pollution-belching, metal locusts that now swarm the giant slabs. With the supply and cost of petroleum and the monumental environmental and capital problems of harvesting which prevents plentiful coal from relieving the pressure, the battery buggy will become more of a rage than in 1900 when a third of the autos in New York City, Boston and Chicago operated on electricity.

Before electricity becomes the number one power choice, alternative fuels, such as ethanol, running in hybrid cars will prepare the way. We are already seeing major automobile manufacturers coming to market with these types of vehicles spurred on by government incentives for research and development.

Fortunes will be made. You can hear it now: "Juice 'er up, sir?"

4. **The Continuing Building Room.** Despite expected high interest rates it seems a foregone conclusion that the building boom will continue, particularly apartments, townhouses and condominiums, albeit at a lower growth rate. The large increase will be among the 25- to 44-year olds, the primary house-forming group, and those 60 and older, the most significant increase in this age group ever. But why will multi-family housing, such as apartments, benefit more than single-family homes? Cost. The prices of single-family homes are rising more rapidly than income. With this trend continuing, a large number of the 30- to 40-year olds will become apartment dwellers, thereby rendering unto multi-family owners (and Caesar) an absolute windfall. If you do purchase an apartment complex, do not treat the tenants as pawns, as the majority of landlords do, but rather as customers. This too will greatly enhance your investment return.

Expect architects concentrating in multi-family dwellings and apartments, makers of institutional furniture, and lamp and mirror manufacturers and the like, to be in the vortex of this market. Space-saving stoves and refrigerators and home entertainment wall systems as well as coin-operated commercial washers and dryers will be in demand.

5. **Nanotechnology.** Nanotechnology is emerging as an explosive growth market. Nanotechnology is defined as the ability to manipulate matter at the atomic level to build microscopic devices

and materials molecule by molecule. Imagine atoms being used to build a working machine! Most know about carbon nanotubes, but consider this: scientists have just created the molecule DTA, which mimics how a human being walks. When heated, linked DTA took 10,000 steps without the assistance of rails or grooves to keep it from deviating off its appointed course.

The industry will become a "T" word in 2015. The national Science Foundation estimates the market for nanotechnology products and services will top one *trillion* dollars by that year in the U.S. alone.

6. **The Migration South**. Climatologists debate whether we are at the beginning of a cycle of global warming. Even though there is evidence the globe is becoming warmer because of rising levels of greenhouse gases (carbon dioxide in Earth's atmosphere, for example, is one hundred parts per million higher than it has been for at least 400,000 years) climatologists believe the Eastern seaboard may actually become colder in winter, not warmer, because thawing sea ice and heavier rainfall in the Northern Atlantic could contribute to cold fronts along that region. Neither our generation nor the next will witness the full extent of such a trend. However, a one or two degree downward tick of the thermometer in our generation (coupled with our energy problem), together with industrial pollution in the North, non-unionization in the South (due to workers' sentiment and the absence of state union shop laws), and an erosion of the tax base disproportionate to the loss of jobs and industry in the northern tier industrial states, could precipitate an acceleration of the movement of people and business to the warmer climates of the South and Southwest. There would be a disorderly migration from the "Frostbelt" to the "Sunbelt." Therefore, a distributorship, bank or other service in Georgia, Mississippi, New Mexico, or Southern California (but not near the Saint Andreas Fault!) might find itself in an increasingly strong growth market.

A petroleum consultant to government and industry, Steven McDonald, who teaches at the University of Texas, asserts that the South's growth will not be affected by the energy shortage for the next two decades. The oil and gas rich Southwest and the coal-rich Border States will actually benefit, he believes, at the expense of the already ailing Great Lakes and New England economies.

When considering a Southern location for the small business, the question arises: Will the South give African-Americans a chance? Part of the answer lies within that population itself. The vast migration of African-Americans from southern to northern cities has all but stopped. Lamond Godwin, southeastern regional director for the National Rural Center, says that blacks, instead of migrating northward, are moving into urban centers in the South. Statistics show that African Americans are leaving the North and West and migrating or returning to the South. Atlanta and Savannah, Ga., Roanoke and Norfolk, Va., Jackson, Miss., Mobile, Ala., and Greenville and Spartanburg, S.C. are experiencing a decrease in white population and an increase in the number of African-American citizens.

African-American perception of improvement in the South, Godwin said, can mean a permanent reversal of historical migration patterns. The Confederate curtain must be raised for long-term prosperity in the South. Many believe it will be.

So, if you can stand chittlins, grits du jour 'en fatback, chewin' terbacky and folks with "red necks," the purchase of a bank, service company, construction company, etc., in the Deep South could be a good investment.

7. **Corporate Governance.** Corporate governance has become a cottage industry with its real opportunity yet to be. The interest in corporate governance actually started prior to July 2002, but the Sarbanes-Oxley Act (SOX) launched the rocket ship. The initial emphasis has been on compliance with SOX, Audit Committees and internal and external accounting.

The "sleeper" section, 301(4), mandating a whistleblower system, is just becoming better known, but the real legacy of SOX will be in putting leadership and entrepreneurship back into the boardroom. And this is what your new consulting business should focus on: how to aid boards in the all-important mission and vision process and how to facilitate director peer review. Neither is mandated by SOX; both are essential for the creation of shareholder value - the real benefit SOX delivers.

There are many other ways your business can put entrepreneurship back into the board room, from risk assessment services to corporate strategy sessions. In no area are the costs so modest and the benefits so substantial, as boards make multi-million dollar decisions on the margin.

8. **Electronic Information Management**. With the advent of e-mail as primary evidence in lawsuits, entrepreneurial opportunities will abound in managing the retrieval and management of this information. For example, witness Document Review Consulting Services, LLC ("DRCS"), an electronic document review and retrieval company for the legal community owned by Huron Consulting Group, LLC. Using double screens at each workstation, DRCS employees organize and interpret a massive number of emails and electronic memos and load them into a database. Each document is then given a keyword for later on-demand retrieval. The documents can then be pulled from the database by attorneys in preparation for discovery and trial at less than half the cost of doing so employing legal associates to retrieve the documents by hand. The savings to law firms (and later to Fortune 500 companies as the service expands to non-legal external users) will be in the millions. DCRS occupies an intriguing new high growth niche.

Seeing row after row of work stations with large double screens conjures up images of London sweatshops of Dickens's time. How ironic that as the Industrial Revolution has been replaced by the Age of Ideas in the business world, hand-done discovery and trial preparation is being replaced by a production line of lawyers!

9. **Growing Replacement Markets.** One can discover many opportunities by studying replacement markets. For example, grand piano sales will explode in the 2000's as will the prices of new and used grands. Because over 30,000 grands were built in the U.S. each year in the 1930s and production subsequently dropped to roughly 12,000 per year from the 1940s until today, demand is on the rise. Using a fifty-year useful life, the grand market replacement need will almost triple. It also helps that grand pianos are the ultimate in the home status symbol whether it is played by the owners or there simply for "show".

An account of the unexpected utility of owning a grand for another, rather un-contemplated and non-musical use (in the traditional sense of "making beautiful music") was once reported by The *London Daily Mail:*

Even to the French, for whom the maximum possible drama is essential in anything to do with love, the divorce case involving Coletta Malondra is extraordinary. A husband was certain that his green-eyed wife Colette was deceiving him. He hired Serge Petremann, a private detective, to gather enough evidence for a divorce. Petremann discovered Colette had three lovers. Under French divorce law, Colette had to be caught in the arms of a lover by a lawyer and a policeman. A trap was set. The husband, the detective, a lawyer and a policeman burst into the villa one day and found Colette alone but something caught the private detective's eye – the grand piano. Petremann strode to it and ordered the suspicious husband to lift the lid. And in the piano's interior, he found the curled-up form of a handsome lover wearing only his underpants. (The question of "boxers vs. briefs" was never answered…)

If this or any other replacement market study in another industry seems irrelevant, then consider investing in a grand piano yourself.

You can put one in your home for $20,000 up to $100,000. With a fifty-year life and a 15% to 20% appreciation expected over the next ten years, where can you find a better investment?

10. **Geriatric Services.** Another new phenomenon is the explosion of the older generation, currently increasing almost twice as fast as the growth of the total population. The ambulatory device (wheelchairs, electric scooters, etc.) and "blue hair" dye businesses will boom, along with ancillary businesses serving an ever-increasing geriatric population. Conversely, the present reduction of the teenage population spells trouble for the makers of station wagons with fold-down back seats, copies of Playboy, mattresses, picnic baskets and prophylactics. But, sales of iPods, computers, cell phones and eye shadow will continue to do well.

11. **Services For the Hearing Impaired.** With noise pollution remaining even as the industrial revolution leaves us, a major growth area in front of us will be anything to aid quality hearing. Whether old or young, there is money in hearing loss. When one couples noise pollution with an aging population, anything having to do with the improvement of hearing will be a growth industry. Services for both the hearing and the hearing impaired will grow exponentially. It is not just the noise level of bands, stereos, traffic, sirens, cell phones, iPods and car stereos that damage the hearing. The hearing-impaired population has rightly received much greater attention and is in the wings to take center stage. Positioned correctly, business can service both the hearing and the hearing impaired while profiting handsomely from this mega-trend.

For the younger to middle-aged population, the recent use of cell phones and iPods threatens to turn eardrums into scar tissue. As in a scene from the famous movie "The Graduate", where Dustin Hoffman was given a tip that "plastics" was the next big thing, hearing enhancement is likely the next mega-growth industry.

Say what?

12. **"Self-Help" Services & Books**. The market for a how-to business book is vast. The number of people in management and self-employment in the world is several billion. It is estimated that there are 20 million entrepreneurs in the U.S. alone. The number of women starting their own business is growing by almost 20% per year. New research shows that 5.6 million people age 50 and older

are now self-employed, a 23% jump from 1990. USA today has reported that the numbers are expected to rise further as baby-boomers seek financial security in their older years.

Those 20 million entrepreneurs would likely buy a self-help book to get them started. Any one of many "take-aways" from the book substantially exceeds the cost of the book to this group. In other words, it would pay for itself in the dividends realized from suggestions that get the business underway. As cheaper and better technology drives down start-up costs, the book would be invaluable to a record number of people. After all, you bought this one, didn't you?

13. **Gotta Love Blonds!** I know a great deal about blonds. I am married to a true blond. I am from a family of eight blonds. Later in life, all of my sisters remain blond with the benefit of a bottle. I am a blond watcher of considerable renown. My curriculum vitae says simply "blond watcher in residence".

One in twenty American women is a natural blond. Blondes reputedly have more fun, look younger, feel sexier and more attractive to the opposite sex. Why else would one in three dye their hair blond? I have spent many a happy idyll in near ecstasy observing this smashing mega-trend, but I've yet to devise a way to make money at it with my mother-lode of blond knowledge. Surely you can...

Chapter 7
Finding and Funding A Small Business

Where To Look For the Small Business

The would-be entrepreneur will also have to weigh two other considerations: where to find a small business for sale and how to raise money to buy it.

Your local commercial bank officer can be an excellent source for locating small businesses for sale. Additionally, he will arrange a meeting for you with the head of the merger and acquisition department of the bank, and with the trust officer handling estate and trust business properties.

You should remind the bank officer that he or she should keep in mind companies with for sale signs like this:

In addition, he or she should re-consider those companies they have previously turned down for loans, or perhaps loans that have turned sour and need infusions of management to turn the operation around.

Other sources for companies for sale can be found in the classified section under "Business Brokerage Firms," or can be obtained from trade associations, your vendors and customers.

Not That Much Money Is Necessary

At first, the most difficult part of purchasing a small business will appear to be the raising of sufficient money. It seems difficult to those of us who have worked for large businesses on a salary while starting out in life, perhaps with a family, and having meager savings and no family wealth. If we had family wealth, we would probably be in the unfortunate position of being the boss's son who turns into the village idiot if the business fails or the boss's son who is given the business on a platter if it is successful. Minimize the need for cash by purchasing a going business or a franchise rather than by starting a business.

Even the best managers can run out of money before the new business can be established. The high cost of starting a business will deplete even a generous bankroll in short order.

On the other hand, consider acquiring a going business, one which was started some time ago and has fortunately survived in spite of the extremely high mortality rate. About 50% of new businesses fail within the first two years, a mortality rate that could be greatly reduced if the Small Business Administration would, as a condition of its loans, place more emphasis on education and managerial ability, thereby making the game a matter of skill, not chance.

Knowing now the obstacles in starting a new business, you can, by lying in wait like a lion for its prey, buy up for a pittance a going business as it struggles during the start-up years. Not only can you minimize the need for cash by purchasing an existing business, you can also bootstrap the purchase. Bootstrapping is simply a method by which a small business is purchased with a nominal down payment, say 10 %, and the balance paid over the long term out of future earnings of the company, not your own pocket. If the business is somewhat cash rich, the deal can be further leveraged by borrowing back the initial down payment from the acquired business. Still it is prudent to have at least six months' to one year's salary in a separate personal reserve over and above any business financing before the purchase.

There are many reasons for selling a business: death, illness, retirement, chance for a better opportunity, tired of it all, a desire to make a profit or avoid going broke. Businesses which are going broke obviously are not best sellers. Buyers are looking for a record of profit, pleasant surroundings and growth opportunity.

Having said this, I suggest rowing into the wind and against the tide. I recommend purchasing a business which is losing money because of poor management but has a service or product with potential. With this *modus operandi,* you will not be competing with other bidders. You will not be paying a multiple of profit. You will solve, in most cases, the need for initial equity money. When you turn it into a winner, you will have shot the moon!

The seller usually wants a sale with installments in future years treated as capital gains in the years they become due.

Anyone prepared to purchase a business with a lot of his own money will try to beat down the seller's price, while you, by negotiating terms, will, ironically, try to "sell" the owner by telling him what an excellent business he has built up, and that his price is more than fair. You are purchasing control, or you, had better be purchasing control if you don't want your second career to be the worst of all possible worlds: working for a family-owned company. The seller might well be unaware that a 51% block of stock in a closely held company is worth more than 51% of the company's total market value. That's because of the ability of the controlling shareholders to elect directors (who, in turn, elect officers), to compensate themselves and set dividends to suit their own purposes - in short, to direct the resources of the corporation to the majority owners' personal advantage. The seller could be losing a premium of anywhere from 20% to 35% by selling a majority interest.

Money Sources For the Small Business Folk

Even though our objective is to purchase a business with a minimum amount of hard dollars, you will still need a general working knowledge of money sources as well as an idea of the cost of money. Small businesses are voracious users of money especially for working capital necessary to support expanding sales.

As a starting point, you need to grip the cold truth barehanded: institutions such as commercial banks, investment banks, savings and loans and even small business investment corporations do not want to lend money to small businesses. This unspeakable truth can never be uttered aloud. It's almost unpatriotic, and the lending companies need the other business, such as your company's checking account, payroll processing business, and employees' savings account. Lending institutions do not want to lend to small businesses because of the high risk and high administrative cost. It takes about the same amount of work to make a $75,000 small business loan as it does to structure a multimillion dollar loan. A large participating loan with other banks is also a piece of cake. And the 4% to 5% rate above the prime rate charged to most small businesses does not counterbalance the risk. If the lender is in search of higher rates, a consumer installment loan at around 25% is available, typically with less risk than a small business loan.

Just how, then, do small business folks draw money from the well? Easy: you shame your banker into making the loan commitment. This is nothing new. Columbus shamed Queen Isabella and King Ferdinand V into financing his hare-brained scheme to substantially reduce the transportation cost of picking up spices and other consumer goods from the Far East. The pay-back to subsequent generations all over the world was huge! He discovered, literally, a whole new world.

Start out like Columbus did. Befriend your patron - your banker. Begin working on this relationship while still under the clueless Mr. Goolsby's tutelage. Start now. Establish a rapport with your commercial banker just like anyone else in the business community. Use your ability, reputation, and candor. Prove that your word is your bond. Do not baby-trade with your banker! Bankers can understand most any human failing except lying and voting Democratic.

After you have established this close relationship you can shame them into lending you the money. Shame being the only motive, you want to make the lending process as painless as possible. Prepare in advance your cash flow projections for the expected term of the loan and pro forma balance sheets with an explanation of how you plan to breathe life into the numbers. Also, show how much money is needed, what it will be used for and how it will be repaid.

Further, suggest alternative methods for making the loans. One of the best is a loan guaranteed by the Small Business Administration (SBA). All funds come from the commercial bank with SBA guaranteeing up to 90 % of the loan to the bank and the bank can set a money market rate within certain limitations. Become somewhat acquainted with SBA regulations. For instance, certain businesses do not qualify, such as publishers, newspapers, casinos, and brothels. Certain loan purposes, such as those made for the purpose of refinancing a debt, make a loan ineligible.

Possible collateral you may use to secure the loan (other than, or in addition to the obvious equipment or building you are financing), as well as your personal financial statements, need to be disclosed. You can expect to be asked for your personal endorsement. This is only fair, since philosophically, if not legally, the business is more an extension of the owner than a separate legal entity.

A direct SBA term loan with a maximum ceiling of $150,000 with all the proceeds coming from SBA would be the most desirable loan because of the artificially low rate. You can count on this SBA rate to be lower than prime, the short-term rate charged most credit-worthy corporate customers even though SBA is lending *term* money from five years for working capital up to 20 years on new buildings. Unfortunately, direct SBA loan applications take a considerable amount of time.

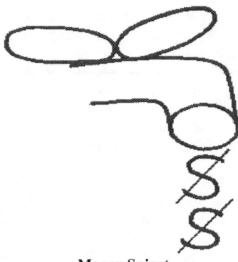

Money Spigot

Also the SBA money spigot on direct loans is constantly being turned on and off. It is my opinion that direct SBA loans will become a budget casualty. Certain loans are given priority from time to time, such as loans in areas declared national disaster areas and loans to minorities and veterans. SBA also has an obligation to create new jobs. Ironically, unless you are adding bricks and mortar, you are trying to get the labor out of your product through efficiency or mechanization, which eliminates jobs!

Another source of funds, small business investment corporations (SBIC's), are privately owned corporations created by Congress in 1958 (with long term debt guaranteed up to three times the SBIC's equity by SBA) expressly to finance small businesses. The purpose was served until the 1967 recession pushed many portfolio companies to the wall or off the wall like Humpty-Dumpty. SBICs have been trying to upgrade their portfolios and increase their yields ever since then by financing larger and sounder companies and demanding onerous equity positions. This background is to let you know that SBICs are not a panacea for your small business money needs.

Borrowing from relatives is not recommended. The emotional coupon is too steep. Doctors and criminal lawyers can be a better source than relatives. Both have the wherewithal to give and take life. (Yes, even the criminal lawyer. If you don't believe he can get you life, just ask him.) Being almighty, there is nothing these two professional groups don't know, including investing in a small business. With their ego and money, you have yourself a money trough. Additionally, because of their high tax bracket, you can provide them a tax shelter, in some instances, if you are purchasing machinery. The professional man purchases new machinery either as an individual or partner and leases to the business at a 20% rate. The investor gets a 10% investment tax credit and accelerated depreciation to shield some personal income from income taxes.

Selling equity is another way to raise money. The major advantage is there is no sinking fund or obligatory pay-back. On the other hand, you will have to give up a piece of the action, and you want to avoid that. You should seek legal advice, if this is considered, to avoid being snared by state and federal security laws.

If all else fails there is always the Mafia, if you can stand the risk/reward ratio. You can let the borrowed principal slide but you had better pay close attention to the interest, unless you want your youngest son to go through life with a non-correctable, artificially crafted hair-lip.

Of all the afore-mentioned sources your commercial banker could be your best bet, Ms. Entrepreneur. He or she can provide factoring, accounts receivable and inventory financing, equipment leasing or financing and handle SBA participation loans, among other things. Your banker can recommend exotic approaches, like a commitment to finance half the seed money with a bank loan guaranteed by SBA with the remainder raised through the sale of common stock to a limited number of people, to name just one example of "creative financing" (See Chapter 4 for more on special tax advantages available to investors in small companies). SBA can guarantee up to 90% of a bank loan up to $500,000. And bankers can put you in touch with the moneyed. Your banker is so important to your success, whether buying or operating a small business, you might want to bring one home to dinner to meet the folks or add a codicil to your will to include him or her.

Specific Examples

Frequently, specific examples are more meaningful than the textbook approach, particularly when explaining how to become a small business owner. Since I've followed the guidelines mentioned earlier in selecting a business, I'll take the witness stand in my own case, knowing the danger of self-incrimination and my legal right to remain silent.

My first job was in commercial banking with Citibank in New York in the national division. Being the proud owner of a new social security number, I began the development of management skills. Banking is a fertile field to cultivate management skills, especially pertaining to marketing, which is more important in banking than perhaps finance. I also learned firsthand about leverage using other people's money. I had made a personal stock investment in a company listed on the New York Stock Exchange through an off-shore brokerage house which required only a 10% margin for the stock purchased. Since I also borrowed the 10% margin I owned about $100,000 worth of stock in 1964 dollars by merely signing my name to a $10,000 note.

In three months, country-come-to-New York had an investment worth $130,000. I was such an idiot; I would brag to my dates that I had a $130,000 portfolio! Suddenly, the bottom fell out of the market when the president dressed down the steel companies for increasing prices. My broker sold my position out at $87,000 without even bothering to ring my phone. Imagine a banker on a regular diet of bologna sandwiches out of a brown bag! Banks are excellent training grounds for managers and Citicorp is one of the best.

During a short stay with Cameron-Brown in Raleigh, North Carolina, my next employer, I became acquainted with the eight stockholders (none of which owned over 30%) of Currier Piano Co., which had just started manufacturing upright pianos in Marion, North Carolina.

For an option on 13% of the stock of a company which really had no worth at the time (instead having substantial losses in the medium six figures) I came to work for Currier at a $7,500 salary, a pittance even for a 26-year-old in 1966.

Pre-tax profits subsequently reached $750,000 in 1972 when Currier was sold. In six years without any investment, the option netted me $995,000. By using the criteria of finding an unprofitable prosaic company with a sound product in an industry with favorable demography, I acquired ownership without any cash investment or debt and made an infinite return on my investment of zero dollars.

How was Currier Piano Company turned around? Currier reduced its 50 piano SKU's (stock-keeping units) to 10 SKU's. How was this accomplished? As was industry practice, each individual Currier piano had a unique body. Each piano had a different dimension and body contour. The decision was made that all spinets (the primary offering) have one dimension and one contour. By virtue of completely changing each upright piano in the shipping department by outfitting them with five different legs, different music racks, bottom panels and piano tops, we were able to offer 50 models but only had 10 SKU's. It looked like we had 50 plus pianos in our line - after all, there were 50 pianos in the catalogue.

Currier, at that time, was the first new piano maker in over two plus decades in a declining industry. We were on the verge of what the old-line companies were predicting: they don't have industry or know-how, and Currier would go the way of all flesh. To the contrary, not only did Currier Piano Company become the largest maker of student pianos in the United States, we became the sixth-largest piano manufacturer and the most profitable on in the U.S.A. to boot!

More importantly, our strategy of disrupting the market by interchanging piano parts to make made-to-order instruments failed to impress the hide-bound, traditional piano industry even after they witnessed our ability to hike profit margins by tripling inventory by a multiple of 3 ½ times. The following year that number jumped to 13 times. With a denominator contracting this substantially, it is easy to understand the increase in ROI (return on investment).

The "rest of the story", as Paul Harvey so famously quipped, was that a great idea first conceived by a bookkeeper at Currier became a major disruptive strategy. It was so significant that only Steinway and Currier survived a later import onslaught by Yamaha and Kawai. Baldwin, Wurlitzer, Aeolian and all the other big names went bankrupt. Kimball, however, survived by exiting through a side door and ducking back into their core furniture business.

IMPORTANT TAKE-AWAYS:

Involve all employees in the disruptive strategy discipline in addition to periodically putting open-ended strategy discussions on the board of director's agenda. I named these board discussions "Chautauqua's," after the philosophical discussions in Upper New York State during the summers in the 1870's. Such exchanges not only gin-up creativity but have the ability to encourage and help employees refine their thoughts with one another. Those ideas create real shareholder value.

Like anything this important, it is challenging mental work, and it will not happen overnight. Like Currier your company could go several years without a breakthrough. (Most companies go a lifetime without a disruptive strategy because all the mental energy is expended on mundane matters, like stock buybacks and other financial machinations; and now compliance box-checking.) But, considering the cost of important disruptive technology, a disruptive strategy will build shareholder wealth equally but at a lesser cost.

GE has already been doing what we did at Currier Piano, except they call it "Dreaming Sessions" as Gary Hamil wrote in *Leading the Revolution:*

> "In most companies there is no distinction between a conversation about radical new possibilities and a conversation about how to squeeze out another percentage point of gross margin. The same standards of analytical rigor are applied to both - whether the subject is the return on a new piece of production machinery or the chance to create an entirely new market. Strategy conversations at GE Capital are labeled "Dreaming Sessions". Questions about internal rate of return and EVA are disallowed. No one mistakes them for budget meetings. A conversation about an opportunity for radical innovation is supposed to be fun, open-ended and inquisitive. It ends with a set of hypotheses to be field-tested. "

It is worth mentioning, however, that GE needs to re-think its strategy of requiring each of its businesses to be first or second in market share. Barriers to competition are falling in the global marketplace. Size and market share are less important today in a highly competitive economic environment than finding new and better ways of doing business.

You will agree, however, that our name, "Chautauqua's", is more descriptive and romantic than GE's "Dreaming Sessions". Whatever the name, my acquaintance, Jeff Emmelt, will take these ideas and GE to a much higher level as the new CEO.

For tax reasons, I invested a good portion of my Currier Piano sale proceeds in public limited partnership oil and gas exploratory drilling ("wild-catting") programs. This made an 80 % intangible drilling write-off available the first year. This investment occurred just prior to the OPEC cartel decision to drive oil prices out-of-sight.

Public oil programs generally have questionable returns, *even considering taxes*. I learned too late that as a rule private oil programs with reputable general partners earn much better returns. Although I erred by investing in public programs rather than private, I was lucky in my timing. The oil programs produced a seven digit net worth for this home-grown turnip.

I didn't learn much from my stock market loss in New York. The only consolation about losing some of the proceeds of sale in the market this time was that the money was not borrowed, and I had been listening closely to Lewis Owen who said, "Living with a loss is folly; taking a loss is wisdom." All my stock investments are now in small companies whose stock is not traded. I have now finally learned that Wall Street is only for professional brokers and traders. If your pension fund or other similar fund owns traded stocks, that's fine, but you and I are at a disadvantage when buying or selling publicly held stock for our own account. You can make much more money owning stock in a small business.

Fortunately, my municipal bond and real estate investments were a little better. One small purchase with the proceeds of the Currier sale was humorous. I bought a $450,000 residential house which the seller knew had termite damage, but I didn't until after I had spent $125,000 on aluminum siding for the entire house. Two years later I was offered $770,000 which I got even after explaining about the termite damage and putting this information in the contract.

I was just as lucky in my acquisition of a seven-year option on 11% of the stock (at a strike price of 10% of net book value) of a textile mill. I simply agreed to endorse a note to purchase new machinery and to serve as a non-paid consultant for two years. The company was breaking even and could not obtain bank financing. The note was prepaid in three years out of profits.

Another purchase was a 32-unit garden apartment complex at a seven-figure cost, borrowing 75% from a savings and loan and all the equity money from a commercial bank. The apartments produce a small book profit and $250,000 a year in non-cash depreciation expenses.

Another transaction which might guide you involved the purchase of 78% of the stock of a lamp and mirror manufacturing company started by Drexel. Stock ownership was *given* to me by the former shareholders in exchange for my agreement to assume the company's bank note, which they had previously endorsed. The bank accepted my endorsement on my word that the note would be paid, and not my worth. My assumption of this debt was predicated on the general creditors forgiving 75% of the company's indebtedness, which they did.

Imagine this opportunity: another money loser experiencing start-up expenses with a product tied directly to the prospects for a housing boom and having a special niche in the market. *And no hard cash necessary!*

As the company turned profitable, it occurred to me that perhaps it would have been better to have allowed the company to be placed in the hands of a bankruptcy court and immediately purchase it from the court. That way, the forgiveness of its debt would have been tax free. Such considerations become important as a company earns income.

In 1979 this same small lamp company with very modest assets and a deficit net worth sold over one million dollars in stock to less than 35 investors and immediately acquired Erwin-Lambeth, an 100 year old premier furniture manufacturer. It still makes furniture the old-fashioned way——on a bench. Both the upholstery and occasional wood factories were leased at $1.10 a square foot for 20 years with no escalation of rent stipulated to by the sellers, which provided additional leverage. Norman Perry, a designer lamp and chandelier company, was also acquired in 1980. Handmade, high quality products and distribution through showrooms and designers with products suitable for affluent homeowners are common to all three companies. With Norman Perry adding accessories, the companies became a single, one-stop resource for the designer and the select high-end retailer. All companies were positioned to benefit from the growth in household formations in the mid and late eighties, the increase of the affluent class, and the swelling demand for high quality.

I was founding CEO of Digital Recorders, Inc. and Pilot Therapeutics Holding, Inc. Both are now public companies, and I earned medium six figure capital gains. Three years after I left Pilot Therapeutics as founding CEO, I had a paper capital gain of almost $3 million dollars. Today, my holdings have a market value of less than $25,000 showing yet again the treachery of publicly traded securities.

As CEO of Data Pix, I had a low six-figure capital loss. As CEO of I.D. Technologies (IDTEK) I lost a high six-figure amount even though both companies miraculously survive! IDTEK was such a rat's nest; it should be the subject matter of a pathology book. I cannot write it because I can't settle on a title. Should it be *"Keystone Kops"*? *"Greed Before It's Time"*? *"You Cannot Build a Technology Company and Defend a Hostile Proxy Fight and Lawsuit For Fraud at the Same Time"*? Any would work...

The future of my directorships and investments in GET Interactive, The Central Lighting Company of California, Clean Technics International, and Remote Light, Inc. will determine if I will be a millionaire a fourth time.

I bare some of my past in this testimony to show you a number of small business acquisitions using the criteria and economic scenarios I've outlined and how to avoid the need for hard cash. And...how to be successful in the process!

You can do all this and more. Now, let's look at how you can manage any small business successfully.

Chapter 8
Live the Sermon

You have arrived. You are now your own boss and basically responsible to yourself and your family. Even though you are putting everything on the line, remember that it is better to starve free than to be a fat slave.

Having made the conversion from being a little fish in a big pond, you now look like this:

Big fish in a little pond

Although it's the crux of success in any business, managerial leadership is not a brief, concise subject. There are managers, who, regardless of what they undertake, will be successful. They have the Midas Touch.

What qualities make these few so successful? To oversimplify, let us say that leadership, motivation, and communication are the ingredients of managerial leadership. Motivation and communication are less important than leadership.

When it comes to leadership, much depends on whether the owner comes from the old school of management theory or from the new school. Does he simply make a decision and then announce it - or does he allow subordinates to make decisions with certain limitations?

Leadership Characteristics: How They Can Be Demonstrated By Example

Walk the Walk

Consistency is a desirable management characteristic. McGregor's Theory Y or Theory X - autocratic versus democratic boss - any management style will work if the manager/owner is *consistent* and leads by example. If your nature is to smile and joke when inspecting the production line or branch store, it can be disconcerting to employees if you come on one day like a Marine drill instructor, barking orders and scolding everyone in sight. On the other hand, if your natural inclination is to be like a Marine drill instructor, you can be just as successful as the easy-going manager, provided you are consistent.

There are four trademarks of one who leads by example: (1) knowing how to listen well, (2) practice saying "no" graciously (3) know yourself and be mentally tough, and (4) don't use your position for personal gain or glory.

Be an eloquent listener.

Most business communications are not public speeches or written memos, but verbal one-on-one communications. The quality of listening attentively is most important. This quality has been developed by a very few. You do not learn when you are talking about why Joe's attitude is a certain way. For that matter, you do not exert leadership because leadership is by example.

Set the example. The subordinate, in turn, will take the cue and listen to his people instead of expounding continually on the way he thinks everybody should be. One of the best ways to lead people is to listen attentively and sympathetically when they come to you with problems and complaints. According to at least one survey, "Of all the sources of information a manager can have that will help him to know and size up the personalities under his supervision, by far the most important is listening to the individual employee. From thousands of workers who liked their immediate superior, the typical report was: I like my boss. I can talk to him. He listens to what I have to say.

The infrequently used and little understood art of listening can change your very life. Since so few possess this attribute, you will immediately stand out and excel without years of practice or preparation. The benefits are enormous. You can learn what is on the other person's mind, and thus can help him solve his problems. Most likely, by talking out the problem, people will also talk themselves into a solution. Thus, it teaches self-reliance at the same time that it makes for better cooperation in implementing the solution to a problem.

Lastly, you have given the person a chance to cool off if he is upset.

Practice the Lost Art of Saying "No" Graciously

Good people in all walks of life -- most especially business people – do not know how to be gracious when telling people no. Only a two letter word, most of us deliver it like one would thrust a dagger into the heart. When speaking to a subordinate, it needs to be delivered as a lingering hug and in a non-threatening way. "No, your idea won't work because..." burns bridges and breaks hearts and spirits. On the other hand, "No, this is well-intentioned but we need to head in another direction..." is neither a dagger to the heart nor a bridge-burner. It preserves dignity and encourages further sharing of ideas.

If there is one thing I want to pass on to my children, it is that you will see many people on the way up and many of the same people on their way back down. I don't mean that one should not explain why "no" was the answer if asked with sincerity, but an explanation need not otherwise be proffered.

Always consider how to deliver the "No" message with the goal of preserving friendship. We all have too few friendships to risk their loss.

Know Thyself

Equally important is your knowledge of yourself, knowing your own strengths and shortcomings.

The most horrible indictment my great aunt would make of a person was, 'He does not know himself." To be a good leader, you must know yourself. Are you a good "morning" person? Do you dislike bankers as a matter of principle? A good leader will know the strengths, weaknesses, preferences, and propensities of his subordinates as well as himself, and will take advantage of them.

The sports editor of a North Carolina daily newspaper once assigned a reporter to cover a major golf tournament—a choice assignment. When asked why he did not cover the tournament, the editor answered, "It would have been a pleasure to cover the tournament, but when I assessed my own strengths and weaknesses, and then his, I knew that I was the better administrator and he the better golf writer, so I gave him the assignment. It was better for our readers." The young sports writer got the assignment, and the sports editor got a raise.

One way to gain insight into yourself is to know your family lineage. It is submitted that searching one's ancestry, which has become almost a national obsession, was kindled by the desire to know ourselves better by looking into our own past. Knowing yourself will improve your ability to lead.

Tough-mindedness is a mental attribute which means that you know what you want and that you have the will and tenacity to get it. Roger Federer and Tiger Woods share this quality, making them almost invincible on the tennis court and golf course. In business, as in the world of sports, this leadership trait can be demonstrated in a number of ways. For example, when you have a prospect that has been solicited by another employee but is leaving the store without buying, you should move onto the sales floor to make that second effort to close the sale. Or, when a new engineering technique has been devised but is not quite what it should be, you should insist that it go back for a re-work.

Don't Feather Your Own Nest

Examples of excesses that dilute leadership abound. Former Secretary of Agriculture Earl Butz epitomized a leader lacking leadership by example. His swollen-belly excesses included a $150,000 paneled dining room for himself and his top aides when there was already a large cafeteria for department people. Butz' penchant for telling racial and off-color jokes offended many minorities and eventually cost him his job.

Even though former Attorney General William Saxbe talked about what he was going to do as a leader, among his first directives was an order for a new, deep-pile gold carpet costing $48,000 because he didn't like the robin's egg blue already in his office. He traveled first class on commercial flights with an entourage of four bodyguards and one public relations man. He also had a chauffeur-driven limousine, his own private dining room near his office and a manservant. During that same time period, the former director of energy, William Simon, continued to be driven in his four-miles-per-gallon limousine, despite the oil embargo.

These are examples of what seems to be criminal lack of leadership by our highest government officials, almost comparable to the excesses of Caligula, the mentally deranged Roman Emperor who killed his father, impregnated and then murdered his own sister and notoriously practiced other debaucheries which would have toppled the Roman Empire had he not been assassinated.

It is important that your personal style create a correct example for your employees. There are no perquisites that should be obvious in the working environment. For example, a free urn of coffee for the office or a luxury limousine purchased by the company is an obvious and visible perk whereas long-term disability insurance, stock options, and bonus plans unavailable to non-management employees are subtle and therefore suitable perks which will allow you to maintain a Spartan and stoical management appearance.

The only thing on the road my limo can't outrun is the swan on the hood

In this respect, one of the most offensive things done by managers in large businesses is to have private parking places with a big reserved name plate in front of the main entrance. This lets employees know immediately that they are inferior to the big shot. The prime parking places should be used by customers or visitors to multiply sales dollars and goodwill.

This is especially true if the business deals directly with the public. It is maddening to patronize a ski resort, furniture store, or discount chain and, after parking in the next county, walk by a dozen parking places reserved for the management people, especially if they are empty! Elimination of private parking would let other employees know that they are not second-class citizens and at the same time build up customer goodwill while creating more sales. It also reminds managers that their primary duty is to preserve and better the firm, not their personal comfort. Self-aggrandizement is a "no-no." If a parking place is so important, one can claim it by being the first on the job!

All offices in a small business should be the same size and have limited decor. The furnishings in each office should be of the same quantity and quality. Visitor chairs in your office should be mildly uncomfortable without arms or cushions. Plush lounge chairs encourage lingering. All offices should be basically utilitarian so as to leave no doubt that the resident spear-carrier is prepared to do combat. This prepares the way for the open office arrangement where the entire phalanx of managers and owners are at identical desks in one large room. This idea will meet strong resistance by those steeped in the big business tradition where rank and class is established not only by office size but also by size of desk, number of windows, thickness of carpet, and so on.

Walking into the Chicago executive offices of a highly structured major corporation to see the chairman and president, a business associate envisioned a celestial-like hierarchy of principalities and powers clustered close to the directors' conference room, complete with thrones, archangels and subordinate angels arrayed in descending order of importance.

Let the quality of your decisions - not your private washroom or the number of wall paintings in your office - establish rank. If you plan a private executive dining room, order Roman loungers and a plates of grapes to enhance the image of managerial decadence to let your customers and suppliers know what "nothings" they are, compared to you. Place your calls through the secretaries, leaving them holding the line for you. You really need a private secretary only to shield you from the real world and provide you with a warm feeling of self-importance.

All the clerical and secretarial personnel should be in a common pool available to all management, including you, the owner. The private secretary so often turns into a personal valet. Things got so bad in one instance in a large firm that a private secretary was actually required to sew up a split in the seat of her boss's pants while he wore them!

The correct procedure is to show all people within the corporate community that the merit system works, that employment is for the benefit of the company and not for each individual to feather his own nest, that management deems itself no better than the working employees, except that their skill of mind is fine-tuned to their task.

All employees are human beings and deserve to be treated as such.

The Right Way...

Take a Spartan approach to management. You must believe in the principle of leadership by example:

- Your company comes first;
- You desire the success of your company;
- You are not going to use your position simply to feather your nest but to further your company's goals;
- You are not better than other employees, save for your orientation to success;
- It is necessary, but not easy, to deny yourself special tangible privileges and other comforts of rank;
- You will displease many people who are seeking companionship and friendship and not success for the company; and
- You cannot be a boss/owner and "one of the guys" too. Someone needs to lead.

Now that you have become an owner of a small business, this Spartan approach is designed so that you could always, in theory, revert to your former status as a grunt without any adjustment or feeling of pain. It is hell to be poor, but worse than hell to be rich and then become poor.

Mix an appropriate level of toughness with your leadership. Your self-image should be like the legendary F-14 Tomcat fighter, perhaps the most recognizable warplane in history. "There's something about the way the F-14 looks, something about the way it carries itself," says Adm. Michael Mullen, the Navy's top officer. "It screams toughness. Look down a carrier deck and you see one of them sitting there, and you just know there's a fighter plane lethal to enemy aircraft."

Examples of True Leadership by Example

G. William Miller, former chairman of the Federal Reserve Board could certainly return if necessary to his humble origins in Borger, Texas, where his father worked in a carbon-black plant after his furniture store failed during the Depression. A big Saturday night in his youth consisted of all nine family members bathing in a washtub in the kitchen (not all at one time, mind you) after which they probably went down to watch the unloading of the A&P truck.

His personal frugal lifestyle continued throughout his stay. While earning a $400,000 annual salary and owning $1.8 million of his company's stock as chief executive of Textron, he continued to live in an unpretentious three-bedroom house without servants. He frequently rode the bus to work and drove a new car for a minimum of six years before trading it in. The closest Mr. Miller ever got to a three-martini lunch was crackers and soup. When I asked Mr. Miller if he shared my conviction that he could return to his humble beginnings without so much as breaking stride, he replied, "My federal job might be all the proof needed."

We all should be able to return to our origins without damaging our outlook on life.

Leadership by example, such as the kind practiced by former President Harry Truman and former Secretary of Labor Peter Brennan, is urgently needed. Truman took public transportation to Independence, Mo., even though some people said he should have flown in the presidential plane to save valuable time. But, Truman knew that leadership by example was essential to the effectiveness of his presidency.

Brennan, the former Secretary of Labor, understood leadership by example. He was a Spartan, and his example rubbed off on the Labor Department. He saved more than $100,000 a month by paring outlays for frivolous interoffice parties and eliminating first-class travel and magazine subscriptions not directly related to Labor Department tasks. He affected additional savings by eliminating some fancy dining rooms and omitting two handball courts from a new Labor Department building.

President Jimmy Carter understood and practiced leadership by example, knowing that even the nation's "huddled masses" relate to actions more than harangues. Following his example, executive branch staff members drove sedans or even VWs, carried their own luggage, and shunned elegant hotel quarters during Carter's tenure in the White House. This had a positive effect on the citizenry.

California's youthful former governor, Jerry Brown, dialed his own phone, flew only tourist class and drove and parked his own sedan while in office. His leadership by example was so strong he lived in a $250 a month apartment in Sacramento to the exclusion of what he considered excess - the state's then new $1.3 million governor's mansion - which he called the "Taj Mahal".

Bearing in mind those instances of governmental leadership by example on both the federal and state level, consider the work style of Robert Wilson, former chief executive officer of Memorex International, a man who breathed life into that ailing computer equipment magnetic-media industrial firm. He drove a Chevrolet Vega to his unassuming office, and he didn't have a private parking place with his name on a metal parking marker. By his example, he non-verbally communicated to each Memorex employee every minute of the day, "Our job is not to make ourselves comfortable or important, not to feather our own nests, but to make money for Memorex. And we all must make personal sacrifices to reach this goal, especially if the personal sacrifices allow other employees to better contribute to Memorex." He was also saying (and he was very aware of this, to be sure) that "You, fellow employee, make a contribution as important as that of the top manager."

Like everybody else, when George C. Seybolt, while president of Wm. Underwood & Co. (now a subsidiary of B&G Foods) came to work in the morning, he went to the time clock, pulled out his time card, and punched in. He marked "trip" and "sick" on the card for days when he was traveling on business or under the weather. This practice of punching in and out—superfluous for executives on salary, not to mention the chief executive officer—is simply a symbolic example and told the workers on the floor that the executives did not elevate themselves above other workers.

No sports coach had more leadership qualities than the late Vince Lombardi, whose ten-year head coaching record with the Green Bay Packers and Washington Redskins included 139 victories, 39 defeats, and four ties. He stressed football fundamentals, superb fitness and mental toughness - and he inspired player participation by his personal example of stoicism and dedication.

Lombardi traveled with his players and lived exactly as they did - no private jets or nights on the town with Howard Cosell. After one game, riding the bus back with the players, Mrs. Lombardi, rarely with her husband during football season, asked where the two of them would eat that night. Unable to believe she would expect special treatment as the boss's wife, Lombardi stood up, waved his arms, and sternly said, "You will eat with the team. When you travel with the team, you eat with the team." She nodded in resignation.

Ho Chi Minh, regardless of his ruthless reputation, understood true leadership to be for the benefit of the followers, not the enrichment of the leaders. Standing in the back of a rice chow line among the troops, he was indistinguishable from the others. Except for the insignia, his uniform was identical to all other North Vietnamese soldiers. Like all other officers, he neither asked for nor exercised any special privileges of rank. He never asked of another that which he could not or would not do himself. He was such an effective leader that he humbled the greatest fighting machine the world has ever known.

There are 300 biographies of Mahatma Gandhi, each with explanations of his power source. When Gandhi was assassinated at age 78 in 1948, Albert Einstein recognized his power source— leadership by example: "Gandhi... demonstrated that a powerful human following can be assembled ... through the cogent example of a morally superior conduct of life." (As an aside, when Gandhi took the Brahmacharya Vow and gave up sex forever, he might have taken leadership by example a bit far...)

If this great country, the bastion of capitalism, is to go the way of the British Empire, it will not be because the working class is supposedly only concerned with pay day and quitting time. Surely, the collapse will be principally the result of lack of management leadership. In the vernacular, management has become soft.

The will to work is very much instilled in the American people. They yearn for leadership. Indoctrination of the virtues of work begins in childhood, is fostered by both parents, and is reinforced even by the children's nursery rhyme:

"Sea saw, Marjorie Daw, Johnnie should have a new master. He shall work for a penny a day because he cannot work any faster."

The working man craves hard work. When you hear a manager say, "People just don't care," the interpretation is really, "I am an ineffective leader. My example is poor. My vision is dim. I am unable to communicate to my people what I want done, and why I want it done and when I want it done."

Management's Erroneous View of the Working Man

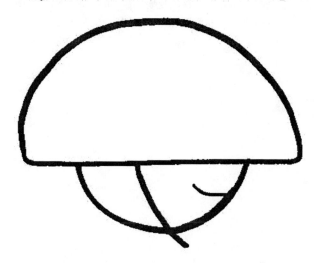

Soldiering on the job in full headgear

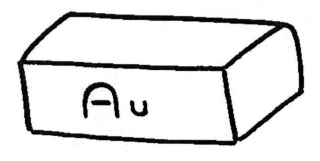

Goldbrick

The growing problem about weakening work attitudes does not lie with the working man. He has been properly indoctrinated, the Christian work ethic runs quite deep, and he is predisposed to hard work. The problem is with the lack of management leadership which management erroneously blames on labor. Labor knows management by what management actually does and by management's style. No amount of words unaccompanied by deeds can convince subordinates of your tough-mindedness.

Try this: Whether you are a lieutenant leading a platoon in Antequitok, a section supervisor designing a new metal stamping machine or manager of the jewelry department, get down with the people. Practice hands-on management. Discuss and communicate the project with them. Exercise leadership. You will be amazed at what can be done. Both productivity and *esprit de corps* will be enhanced. Profits will soar.

Chapter 9
Managing Time

Death is a fact. Every man and woman, every living creature in the world, comes eventually to the moment of death. As far as we can determine, the inevitability of death causes no anxiety to trees, turtles or blackbirds. Only man seems to be aware of death as a part of his future, and it would appear that only man is afraid of it.

Because of death, all of us, manager, or laborer, priest or lawyer, black or Frenchman, have a limited, infinite number of hours to achieve our goals, and this time is not refundable. Our appointed working lifetime is less than 160 quarters. It is important that each of us use this precious gift wisely.

In our younger days we always pretended to be older than we were so we could buy intoxicating spirits, get into forbidden clubs and watch more "interesting" movies at the Cineplex. But when one gets along toward the mid-forties, we tend to start counting from the other end.

Time is our most valuable resource. We need to establish a schedule for developing entrepreneurial management skills while with a large company, skills such as the time needed to select a small business, the time needed to get our small business in order, and the time needed for planning succession.

Even though most large businesses are excellent training grounds for the development of management practices, you don't want to remain there for more than five years simply because the energy of youth is needed when you begin a business of your own.

So, let us budget five years (about 13 % of our working life) to the development of management skills, knowing that any ill-advised decision during the training years will be at the expense of the monolith and Mr. Goolsby. Our search for a suitable small business will take about one-and-a-half years. Using this full-time frame is extremely important in order to avoid making an irrational decision on a second career.

After the transition to entrepreneur, your first three critical years as a small business owner will be an excellent training ground in the use of your time. You should reserve adequate time for your family, for exercise and for reading of a general nature—in that order—but, all other time should be applied to the administration and operation of your new business during the demanding first three years as owner.

Your family has first right to your time and you will want to honor this call. If you ever need incentive, one might remember the father who, after many years of ignoring the wishes of his son, found, in later life, that he had overlooked what was most important to them both, as poignantly articulated in a poem by Debra D. Barone:

To My Grown-up Son

My hands were busy through the day,
I didn't have much time to play.
The little games you asked me to do.
I didn't have much time for you,
I'd wash your clothes, I'd sew and cook,
But when you'd bring your picture book
And ask me please, to share your fun,
I'd say, "A little later, Son."
I'd tuck you in all safe at night, and
Hear your prayers, turn out the light,
Then tiptoe softly to the door.
I wish I'd stayed a minute more, for life is short,
And years rush past. A little boy grows up so fast.
No longer is he at your side,
His precious secrets to confide.
The picture books are put away.
There are no children's games to play.
No good-night kiss, no prayers to hear.
That all belongs to yesteryear.
My hands, once busy, now lie still.
The days are long and hard to fill.
I wish I might go back and do,
The little things you asked me to...

However, some of the non-productive time spent watching baseball, sleeping late on Saturday morning, daydreaming in the shower, reading the Sunday comics....an occasional afternoon delight…and chewing fat at the corner drug store will have to be curtailed for your family and business during the first three years or so in your new-found career.

Eat, drink, and be merry, for tomorrow we die…Ecclesiastes 8:15

During the first three critical years as a small business owner, you will be forced into making some decisions as to the use of time, and you will not find it very helpful just to sit twirling your worry beads. Don't think of delegating authority as simply having a problem or having a letter come in and asking a subordinate to answer it or solve an issue it raises. The most effective way to manage your time is to be sure that the subordinate does not shift his problems to you. You might use the paper clip inventory, in your desk drawer as a gauge of effective delegation - if you are continuously replenishing your paper clip inventory you probably are shifting the problems to the "spear-carriers."

If you are trying to manage time effectively, you will keep the monkey on their back, so to speak, by responding, "Yes, you are right! I'll be interested in what you have to recommend in the way of answers to the problem. Give it your time and attention. And when you have your possible answers, let me know your decision."

Each of us has a most productive time of day and you will want to ascertain that time, if you haven't already. Don't allow this time to be used by others. Use it for your major policy considerations. This does not mean to get off to yourself and read memos but to take care of the high priority items such as thinking through policy or discussing important matters with a certain cadre in your small business. Remember, during this productive time schedule no run-of-the-mill visits, business or otherwise, and have all calls held. Afterwards gather up and gang tackle all the calls. Then see the visitors you have scheduled.

Another recommendation for saving time is to file all general articles and non-pressing correspondence for reading on your next trip away. You can cut through this material on your next flight or in your motel room in short order. And don't be surprised at how even a small lapse of time makes a number of items suddenly unimportant.

Although we have touched on how business meetings waste time, especially in big business, it is nevertheless helpful for a small business to have one formal management meeting per month, say, on the first Monday in the month after the previous month's internal financial statements are completed. The monthly meeting is to exchange information, not to make decisions. Meetings became a way of life for Lenin and his colleagues in Switzerland leading up to the Bolshevik Revolution. John Kenneth Galbraith wrote in *The Age of Uncertainty* that one does not hold conferences to make decisions but "to proclaim shared goals; to show the participants that they are not alone and therefore to improve the morale of the conferencees".

A decision, not to be confused with a consensus, is best made after individual discussions, not in a meeting. The oft unstated-but-understood purpose of a decision-making meeting is to say what the boss wants to hear and to establish that he is boss. Many such meetings are lengthy because of the probing necessary to discover what the boss wants to hear. When one spends his entire time saying, "Yes, sir!", "By all means, sir!" is he truly contributing to the decision-making process or merely helping establish who is the chief? Many decision-making business meetings have the latter as an unstated purpose.

Remember the advice of Sam Goldwyn of Metro-Goldwyn Mayer:

"I don't want to be surrounded by yes-men. Say "No!" every now and then ... even if it costs you your job."

In your one monthly meeting, each manager should give a critique of what has happened in his bailiwick since the last monthly meeting and describe the different ideas or plans being considered in his area of responsibility. In short, give a preview of things that might require a decision after, but not in, the meeting. The manager should then conclude with his or her three biggest problems, three biggest opportunities, and three highest specific corporate priorities. Making money, for example, is too general a priority even for the owner; rather, a marketing study on a new mall (which is to produce money) is more within the meaning of priorities.

By limiting your company to one meeting a month – unless there is absolutely no other practical way to share information - the single biggest waste of time in the business world will be avoided.

If you find that, God forbid, more than one meeting is necessary, at least keep the following in mind:

1. Hold the number of members to a minimum.

2. Stay only as long as you need to make your contribution.

3. Schedule an ending time as well as a starting time and stick to the schedule. If this doesn't work insist that everyone in the meeting stand up. Everybody will swear you're demented, but you won't go limp and faint from exhaustion in another business meeting.

4. Meetings scheduled one-half hour before lunch or dinner often last only one-half hour.

If a subordinate asks to drop in your office for a few minutes, another useful technique to manage time is to say you'll come to his office instead. That way you can choose when to go see him, and, more importantly, when to leave his office. You're in control of time, not him. Moreover, you have paid him a handsome compliment by coming to him.

During your first three years you will find that the telephone can save you a tremendous amount of time, particularly in lieu of written correspondence, which is greatly overdone. Typed letters have become more expensive than a phone call with the surge in clerical wages. The telephone, E-mail, and personal handwritten notes will do just fine until you grow larger.

Be sure that you use the telephone for delivering messages and not for idle conversations. Make a rough outline of the substantive matters you wish to discuss. Call back rather than hold your party up while looking for an answer - and call just before lunch, if you have trouble terminating conversations. This way the party will terminate the call for you.

Even though I am a lone voice crying in the wilderness, I suggest dialing your own calls rather than having your secretary dial them. I realize that a secretary can dial as well as you can at substantially less cost per minute, but this technique is extremely offensive. Considering the enormous amount of money spent on advertising to create goodwill, and with the idea of keeping a stoical approach, one would think it would be worth the investment in time to dial his or her own calls to customers or clients.

If you *really* wish to save time using the telephone, you might try this automatic answering device:

Reprinted by permission of the Chicago Tribune-New York News Syndicate

Whereas the first three years put the business on a successful course, you can expect, in the next five years, to constantly run the business on a day-to-day basis, but you will be less "doing" and more "overseeing" – delegating, as the manual says. Now, knowing achievement in small business is a mountain to climb, not an escalator to ride, you are entitled to savor your success.

The subsequent five to ten years will require little day-to-day supervision if you have groomed the right management team. You can then spend time on special projects such as a favorite charity, coaching Little League, getting your handicap back down and maybe even a bit of cruising on e-Harmony.com.

During the latter phases, do not overlook the need for training a successor. Unlike the owner who is best reconciled to the finality of time and death, your corporate charter says your company's life is not finite, but unlimited. Hence, devote needed time to succession planning.

Chapter 10
Of "Yes Men" and Yellow-billed Oxpeckers

Unfortunately, the three-tier hierarchy of all incorporated businesses - stockholders, directors and officers - is the same in smaller corporations.

Failing to pay attention to the three-tier hierarchy can cause legal problems. Company creditors can disregard the separate entity of the corporation and attack the personal assets of the shareholder/owner. Officer compensation, normally deductible by the corporation, can be declared non-deductible dividends by the corporation.

By following the right form and delineating capacity, your attorney-of-choice can circumvent these legal problems. But the primary reason for paying attention to the three-tier hierarchy, especially directors and the corporation's officers, is to better manage the business, and your attorney surely cannot help you here.

Except for frequent failures in long-range planning, the typical small business suffers most (compared to big business) in failing to put emphasis on organization. The just-beginning management glut makes organization even more important. With substantially more junior executives, the scarce senior executive will have to be more explicit and comprehensive in job descriptions, with less time to guide the junior executive through assignments by tutoring. This failure lies not only in the realm of forming an organization chart, but in making formal job descriptions for every job, putting together good resumes and salary histories, and evaluating the potential of every manager and director.

In addition to a detailed job description on every management and staff person, a general job description should appear on a line-and-staff organization chart, such as the one on the following page.

LINE - AND - STAFF QUICK READ ORGANIZATION CHART WITH BRIEF JOB DESCRIPTIONS

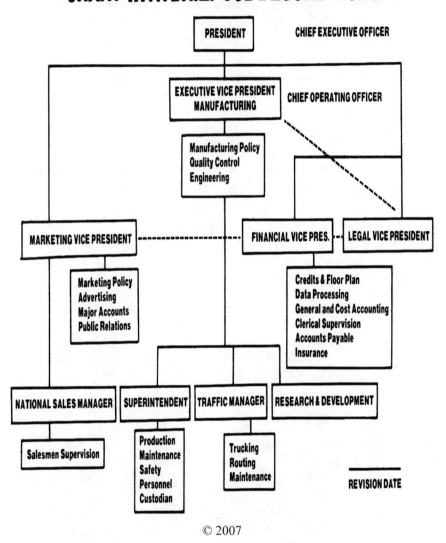

© 2007

This hybrid line-and-staff organization chart and brief general job description (introduced by the author especially for small business) is innovative in that general job descriptions, heretofore articulated separately in written form by job, are given graphic presentation. By incorporating a general job description into the organizational chart, the reader is given an instant, clear snapshot of the organization.

Four management tiers have been created, even though they may not constitute actual line authority from one person to another in a different tier. For example, although the executive vice president ranks two tiers above the national sales manager, the executive vice president has no authority to dismiss or to give a salary increase to the national sales manager. The tier concept is helpful as a way of allocating time, with the higher tier management being given more time and priority for the consideration of such policy matters as salary and fringe benefits administration, long-range planning and budgeting, new products, organization, and the like.

The designation of chief executive officer (CEO) means *numero uno*. Harry Truman said it with his famous plaque, "The buck stops here."

The CEO usually has the title of president and is responsible for the mission and organization of the company through leadership by example, a responsibility he accomplishes principally by means of effective leadership.

The New Yorker Magazine. Inc.   Drawing by Richter; 1970

The CEO is accountable to the board of directors. (Reference "DMZ" article in supplement) The directors of a small business should be selected on the basis of experience and competency, which means that relatives and in-laws typically do not qualify.

The directorships should come from the business community, from among those who are successfully managing other businesses. These persons need not be in a similar business or industry but must learn your business and industry. Stock ownership of your company is not necessary.

Your CPA, attorney and investment counselor should not be considered as directors, for their input is already substantial, and the directors may decide to reshuffle the outside professional people at some future time.

UNDERSTANDING THE CORPORATE STRUCTURE OF BIG BUSINESS

CHAIRMAN OF THE BOARD
Leaps tall buildings in a single bound
Is more powerful than a locomotive
Is faster than a speeding bullet
Walks on water
Gives Policy to God

PRESIDENT
Leaps short buildings in a single bound
Is more powerful than a switch engine
Is just as fast as a speeding bullet
Walks on water if the sea is calm
Talks with God

EXECUTIVE VICE PRESIDENT
Leaps short buildings with a running start & favorable winds
Is almost as powerful as a switch engine
Is faster than a speeding BB
Walks on water in an indoor swimming pool
Talks with God if special request is approved

VICE PRESIDENT
Barely clears a Quonset hut
Loses a tug-of-war with a locomotive
Can fire a speeding bullet
Swims well
Is occasionally addressed by God

ASSISTANT VICE PRESIDENT
Makes high marks on the wall when trying to leap buildings
Is run over by locomotive
Can sometimes handle a gun without inflicting self-injury
Dog paddles
Talks to animals

ASSISTANT CASHIER
Runs into buildings
Recognizes locomotives two out of three times
Is not issued ammunition
Can stay afloat with a life preserver

ASSISTANT SECRETARY
Falls over doorsteps when trying to enter building
Says, "Look at the choo-choo"
Wets himself with a water pistol
Plays in mud puddles
Mumbles to himself

SECRETARY!!
Lifts buildings and walks under them
Kicks locomotives off the tracks
Catches speeding bullets in her teeth and eats them
Freezes water with a single glance
SHE IS GOD!!!!

The use of company managers inside your business as directors should be avoided because of the "Yes, sir" tendency. The outside executives who are successful in other firms are going to speak their beliefs and experiences readily and freely.

Directors' meetings should be held each quarter, with director information mailed as it comes up and not accumulated until the quarterly meetings. Any major decision requiring a study should be mailed to each director ten days prior to the meeting.

Five, maybe seven, directors are a workable number, and their pay per meeting should be enough to attract them. If you say you can't afford this, I have to tell you that you can't afford not to pay it because of the substantial return this caliber of directors will give your business.

The designation of a chief operating officer further refines the organizational framework by designating responsibility for execution of corporate policy, in this case, to the executive vice president. The chief operating officer could be, of course, the general manager or superintendent - or he might hold any similar title - and is most frequently the number two person in the company. These designations assume more importance as your business grows and prospers. Maybe one day you, too, will become a giant company and will need a detailed description of each title.

The line-and-staff relationship evidenced by dotted lines in the illustration is the most popular form of business organization, borrowed from the military. It relies on the use of specialists in all lines attached to the various branches - a psychologist, for example, in every division. Stanley M. David, co-author of *Matrix,* says, "The solid and dotted-line relationships are like an executive ménage à trois with one legitimate relationship and one illegitimate." As your small business grows, you need to make both legitimate.

Line authority, as shown by the solid line between the president and marketing vice president, makes it clear that the boss is responsible for the welfare of the subordinate. Conversely, the subordinate is responsible for carrying out his duties listed in the job description and to be his boss's alter ego. The many that lose sight of this latter function make mediocre employees at best.

A good subordinate is like the Yellow-billed Oxpecker which lives on the back of a rhinoceros, keeping the rhino free of blood-sucking ticks and warning of impending dangers by flying up with rattling cries.   Next time you want to really compliment a subordinate, call him a Yellow-billed Oxpecker.

The dotted line in the chart designates a staff relationship among management people.   The legal vice president is in a staff relationship with the executive vice president, whom he is charged to assist. He, as shown by the solid line, reports directly to the president, who gives him more bread, who metes out crumbs and who also can turn his bread to milquetoast if he fails to do the job.

The legal vice president, then, only has one boss designated by the solid line but advises and counsels certain other managers. As an additional example, the legal vice president could be called on by the marketing vice president to assist in a potential Magnuson-Moss Consumer Warranty Act violation. Even though a line-and-staff relationship could be created between, say, the superintendent and the legal vice president, an EEOC discrimination problem needing legal guidance would be channeled from the superintendent through the executive vice president to the legal vice president. Although more time consuming, this method has the overriding advantage of making the executive vice president aware of the problem, which, after all, is his responsibility.

This does not mean that cooperation should not be given by all management people to others regardless of the tier, particularly in a small business environment. To the contrary, the chief executive is responsible for administration, motivation and interaction among all company people, and discord might be channeled through the president back to the bosses of the people involved. Smoke, in other words, will be brought to bear.

The line-and-staff plan eliminates the necessity for each manager to be highly competent in each phase of his job - legal aspects in this instance - while preserving the advantage of making each person at any level responsible to a single boss.   Put pedantically, it incorporates the principles of division of labor without foregoing the important link between authority and responsibility.

Concerning resume, salary history and evaluation, the management inventory record on the following two pages is complete:

MANAGEMENT INVENTORY RECORD

Photo

BIOGRAPHICAL DATA

1. Name _____
2. Birth Date_____ Date of Employment_____
3. Sex _____ Marital Status _____
4. Citzenship_____
5. Age(s) of Dependent Children _____

EDUCATIONAL DATA

6. Highest School Grade Completed:

High School	University
8 9 10 11 12	1 2 3 4 5 6 7 8 +

7. Academic Training

College or University	Major Courses of Study	Degree Received	Year of Degree

8. Language _____

9. Branch of Service _____
   (Army, Navy, Air Force, etc.)

10. PROFESSIONAL DESIGNATIONS

_____

_____

11. Three Year (or since employment)
    Compensation History

Date of change	Salary	Bonus/Date	Total

12. WORK EXPERIENCE (Start with most recent job)

Dates	Firm and Location	Job Title	Nature of Assignment	Highest Salary	Reported to (Name-Title)

PERFORMANCE EVALUATION

13. Rate the following Personal, Current Position and Growth Potential Attributes
of the Individual (CEO to complete).

	Do Not Wish To Rate	Poor ——		Average ——		Outstanding ——
Personal						
Communication Abilities	_____	1	2	3	4	5
Relations w/Peers/Subordinates	_____	1	2	3	4	5
Objectivity	_____	1	2	3	4	5
			Total and Average:			_____
Current Position						
Job Knowledge	_____	1	2	3	4	5
Quality of work	_____	1	2	3	4	5
Quantity of work	_____	1	2	3	4	5
Initiative	_____	1	2	3	4	5
Judgment	_____	1	2	3	4	5
Results vs Objectives	_____	1	2	3	4	5
			Total and Average:			_____
Potential for Growth						
Planning & Organ. Talent	_____	1	2	3	4	5
Peripheral Job Interests/ Knowledge	_____	1	2	3	4	5
Business/Profit Orientation	_____	1	2	3	4	5
Line Management Talent	_____	1	2	3	4	5
Staff Management Talent	_____	1	2	3	4	5
Expertise w/Customers	_____	1	2	3	4	5
Peer Acceptance if Promoted	_____	1	2	3	4	5
To Replace His Supervisor	_____	1	2	3	4	5
			Total and Average			_____

Using the formal organization chart with a general job
description designated on the chart itself and the management
inventory record, any reader can gain an immediate understanding of

how the organization works. Just as our organization chart combines the chart and job description, so does the management inventory record contain a resume, salary history and evaluation of each manager. Your outside counselors, such as bankers, attorneys and directors, will be interested in both these resources while internally only the formal line-and-staff organization chart needs to be understood by all, including the non-exempt employees. You might consider permanently posting the organization and job description chart in the corner of the company bulletin board discussed later in Chapter 11.

Now you have the problem of what to do with your old Spider organizational chart as conceived by Leon Danco in *Beyond Survival.*

The Spider Form of Organization Chart

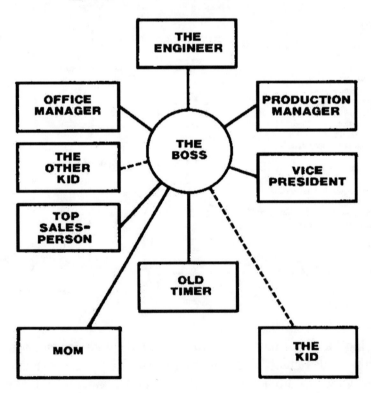

Regardless of the disposition of this chart, or, more importantly, the son-in-law's competency and ability, the son-in-law will never receive rank, or even equality, with the son, who alone has claim to rights of primogeniture.

First of all, the son has been in the sandbox longer, and secondly, Big Daddy cannot overlook the fact that the big lug son-in-law is intimate with his sweet baby girl, and, who knows, he might one day divorce her.

This may be the most typical small business organization chart. It is counterproductive in that all problems, even those solvable by minimum-wage clerical help, belong to the boss. Minor matters consume time which should be spent on major matters involving profit or loss consequences. Of course, for a high-level manager to have nine people reporting to him is not workable under any circumstances, as Eastern Air Lines with 14 senior executives reporting to Chairman Frank Borman soon learned. But, even this archaic "spoke" organizational chart has one feature which, subconsciously, Big Daddy might need: he feels awfully important with nine people fighting over his time. The higher rank of the oldest son is unquestionable, and, where the boss has more than one son, primogeniture gets the nod, even if the older is a despicable alcoholic and the angelic younger is a mathematical-management whiz kid.

Although more prevalent in big business, the "assistant to" is another organizational chart which can smother the life out of any small business.

When executives are engaged in ego empire-building, they frequently overstaff and authorize numerous, inefficient "assistants to". Equally troublesome is senior management using corporate resources for internal purposes. The corporate must be external and should be structured for the customer. There is no business without a customer.

To underline this, the CEO must answer his or her own phone. Ken Thompson, Chairman, President and Chief Executive Officer of Wachovia Corporation, makes it a point to do so in order to be accessible to and stay in touch with the customer.

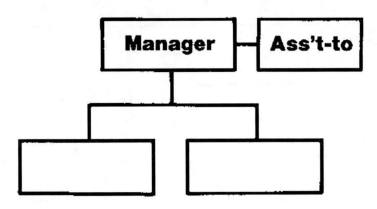

The function of the "assistant-to" can best be appreciated by the story of a woman who went into a pet shop to buy a parrot. "Here's a fine talking bird," said the salesman. "For years he was kept in the office of an assistant-to. Weren't you, Polly?" "Yes, sir!" shrilled the parrot. "Oh yes, oh yes, oh yes, sir! Yes, indeed, you're absolutely right! Yes, sir!"

The "assistant to" is created by a manager who cannot deal directly with his subordinates. Instead of direct confrontation with the boss, which is essential, a subordinate gets meetings with and memos from the "assistant to" - a cause of endless foul-ups. Eventually the Yellow-billed Oxpecker will not hear the impending danger as a result of crossed wires, or, worse, the boss in all this confusion might not hear the clamorous warnings of the Oxpecker.

Chapter 11
Selecting Management People

Administration of management personnel of a small business will become easier. Not because we will have better understanding of what makes Sammy run, but because of our oversupply of quality management people. This oversupply cannot be absorbed into the economy any time in the next decade if the national economy continues to grow at only 3.5 % annually. Moreover, it may be that we will be unable to achieve even this historic growth rate in the future. Axiomatically, the price of management will remain suppressed while the supply of management exceeds demands, as has been described earlier.

There are, however, certain basic principles on which the person in charge can rely. He or she might remember, first of all, that the most dependable guide to the future (in this case the future behavior of a subordinate) is the past, especially when making a determination of ethics, the most important hiring consideration.

As Patrick Henry said, "I know of no way of judging the future but by the past." There is a deep consistency in the human personality. The past, to use an extreme example, can be used to predict a person's reaction to dying. A person facing death will not change the learned reaction to stressful situations.

A person who has been told he has a debilitating disease and reacts by heavy drinking will give a similar response if he is fired (a misfortune a small business owner never faces, you'll be glad to learn.) Someone else who loses a job might turn around and say, "Those bastards are not going to get me down," and go out and acquire his own successful business.

Before a job interview takes place, you can learn of the applicant's success as a manager by delving into his past. Calling references, former employers, former friends, and former enemies can give you tremendous insight into the likelihood of the success of the applicant, for the consistency of business personality runs deep and certainly repeats itself.

There are other things that can be learned simply by reading a resume. In applying for a warehouse supervisor's job, one applicant lost his chance by the careless use of language when he wrote about some very inappropriate prior experience on his resume. Or, there might be evidence that the person is over-educated for the particular job. Business is more an art of finding information than statistical problems requiring equations and giant mental gymnastics. As Thomas A. Murphy, former chairman of GM, said, "Drama in business lies mostly in doing well the job right before you." An over-qualified person is likely to be an unfulfilled employee. A PhD in political science, for example, is likely to be an unhappy store manager for A&P unless, of course, you delve into his past, as in the case of this English guest:

All his life, a dignified English barrister-widower with a considerable income had dreamed of playing Sandringham (one of Great Britain's really exclusive golf courses), and one day he made up his mind to chance it when he was traveling in the area. Although he was well aware that it was very exclusive, he asked at the desk if he might play the famous course. The secretary inquired, "Member?"

"No, Sir."

"Guest of a member?"

"No, Sir."

"Sorry," the Secretary said.

As he turned to leave, the barrister spotted a slightly familiar figure seated in the lounge, reading the Times. It was Lord Welleby Parham. He approached and bowing low, said, "I beg your pardon, 'Your Lordship, but my name is Higginbotham of the London law firm of Higginbotham, Willoughby and Barclay. I should like to ask a huge favor. I wonder if I might play this delightful course as your guest."

His Lordship gave Higginbotham a long look, put down his paper, and asked,

"Church?"

"Episcopalian, sir. And my late wife, Church of England.

"Education?" the old gentleman asked.

"Eton, sir, and Oxford - magna cum laude."

"Athletics?"

"Rugby, sir, spot of tennis, and rowed number four oar on the crew that beat Cambridge."

"Military?"

"DCCE, sir, Coldstream Guards, Victoria Cross, Knight of the Garter."

"Campaigns?"

"Dunkirk, El Alamein, Normandy, sir."

"Languages?"

"Private Tutor in French, fluent German, and a bit of Greek."

His Lordship considered briefly, then nodded to the Club Secretary and said: ... *"Nine holes."*

In reading a resume, consider it favorable for small business if the educational background is in liberal arts. A generalist required for success in small business is more of a Renaissance man than a technocrat. Of course, if it shows that the applicant is a Harvard Business School graduate, be assured that he wants not *a* job, but *your* job.

The applicant's scholastic record is germane. Gentleman C is passé. A high class rank from a respected college or university is indicative of probable success in the business world. Because of the recent trend for giving many A's and B's to students who would have received lesser grades even a half decade ago, class rank has become central. Remember, academic success indicates tenacity, ability to establish priorities, search out facts and ability to think problems through.

A resume will usually give a clue to the person's religious affiliation, and I have found it useful to gain insights from a pastor or rabbi about an applicant.

A resume often indicates an only child, which some employers avoid.

The interview with the applicant is very important because in the business world first impressions gained from first meetings are all too lasting. The typical business transaction is conducted with people who are meeting for the first time or people who have no enduring relationship with each other. Your reaction to the person the first time around is useful as a way of judging how other people will view him when they first meet him.

Over-aggressiveness, verbosity, lack of clarity in expressing views, a tendency to lecture the interviewer, be overly critical of employers and, again, poor grooming and dress should be enough to short circuit any further consideration. Observe the applicant's nervous twitches, eye contact and any negative body language, for the business world is tuned to such nuances of behavior. John Wesley Hardin, the old-time Texas gunman, said he never watched an opposing gunfighter's hands when in a dangerous situation; he watched his opponent's eyes, for a person's eyes, he said, communicate his thoughts and tip off his actions.

You will also find it helpful to meet the applicant's spouse since he or she will become a silent partner in your business. If it can be arranged, meet the applicant's children and even parents. Observing them will give you a deep insight into the likelihood of the applicant's success. You can count on seeing the applicant's family on occasions in a small business.

There are certain spouses, whether male or female, who virtually guarantee their partner's failure. You know the type: the spouse who dominates the partner, whose every statement is calculated, who is completely wrapped up in one's self, and who insists on answering questions directed to the spouse. In the end, the spouse will almost literally press the life out of the partner by constant nagging. Livia's feeding of poisonous figs to Augustus Caesar was more humane. Feel sorry for your petitioner, but don't hire him. You are a capitalist, not a social worker.

Most large businesses administer aptitude tests to management applicants to provide an indication of the applicant's probable success. The brilliance of big business in administering these tests is awe-inspiring to us small business folk who have heretofore trusted our inquiry into the applicant's tenacity, character, and stoicism. An example of the high esteem I have for such tests might best describe my feelings. My favorite is the Trivia Ineptitude Test of Stanford. This aptitude test is sold on a subscription basis to the biggies at a $4,000 fee, but you now have it free for your small business.

Here it is:

1. In 1830 the exchange which grew into the New York Stock Exchange had its slowest trading ever. How many shares changed hands?

2. What is the oldest business school in the United States?

3.   In how many days did Eli Whitney devise the machine that rapidly separated the fibers of short-staple cotton from seed?

4.   Name the farmer whose idea of barbing wire fencing in 1874 made possible effective management of range lands, and speeded settlement of the West.

5.   What was the record low interest rate on long-term government bonds in United States history?

6.   Which president warned that "Inflation is worse than Stalin"?

7.   What prominent underworld figure bargained with the United States government and received his release from prison and deportation to Sicily by virtue of his influence over the longshoremen and their subsequent aid in monitoring the movement of German submarines, thus aiding in the winning of World War II?

8.   What prominent banking firm for years advertised "We are not incorporated," thus taking full advantage of the personal liability aspect of a partnership to secure business?

9.   Upon organizing the assembly line in automobile production, Henry Ford shocked the industrial world – and heard his competitors claim that he would go out of business - by promising to pay an outrageously high and unheard-of rate of pay?

10.   "Damn the public!" was a statement in response to consumer inquiries (similar to modem-day consumerism in regard to big business). Who said it?

11.   In the days of the Old West, chances were good that the familiar wooden Cream of Wheat container would be useful for what purpose when the cereal was gone, as documented by at least one famous painting?

12.   If the average modem businessman were paid at the exchange rate used in Biblical times, would one gold talent a year be an adequate salary?

13.   The collectivization of land into more efficient, large-scale plots for agricultural purposes has usually been an

important step in the process of becoming an industrialized nation. What best-seller by John Steinbeck dramatically portrays the displacement of farmers during the 1930s by the tractor?

14. According to the Malthusian Theory, when the labor force is reduced suddenly, real wages go up temporarily. What catastrophe in 1665 in Europe actually lent proof to this theory?

15. What was the highest individual income tax ever imposed?

16. Phil, the Fiddler, and Rugged Dick were stereotyped heroes who epitomized the American success story. Who wrote the melodramatic books about them?

17. What was the first artificial waterway in the United States that was an instant financial success?

18. What presidential candidate ran on a Democratic platform calling for nationalization of railroads and telephone companies and a graduated income tax?

19. Give the name of the industrialist who threw a lavish party in 1886 on his 7,000-acre estate in Tuxedo Park, New York. He also designed for his son, Griswold, an outfit for the party distinguished by its dress coat without tails and waistcoat of scarlet satin. It remains the accepted formal men's dress.

20. Before World War I, executives of big business had become a recognized group deeply affecting the character of American society. Over the next fifty years, what was the percent increase in numbers of this group?

Answers to Aptitude Test
1. 31
2. Dartmouth's Amos Tuck School of Business Administration (1901)
3. Ten days.
4. Joseph Glidden.
5. 1.95 %.
6. Herbert Hoover.

7.   "Lucky" Luciano.
8.   J. P. Morgan & Co.
9. $5 per day.
10. George Vanderbilt.
11. A mailbox.
12. One gold talent would equal a salary of $30,000.
13. *The* Grapes *of Wrath.*
14. The bubonic plague.
15. 91 % in the war years of 1944-45.
16. Horatio Alger, Jr.
17. The Erie Canal.
18. William Jennings Bryan in 1896.
19. Pierre Lorillard IV.
20. More than 400 % in number, or, more than twice as fast a the national population growth.

This test, like aptitude tests used by large companies, will give you no hint whatsoever of the applicant's potential success, but 14 or more correct answers will indicate that he is overly concerned with the nitty-gritty of business. Just maybe big business deserves this anal personality. . .

When all else fails, you may resort with clear conscience to the "horror-scope" method for selecting management personnel. Simply ask the applicant's birthday, and check it against these horror-scopes:

Aquarius (Jan. 20 - Feb. 18) - You have an inventive mind and are inclined to be aggressive. You lie a great deal. On the other hand, you are inclined to be careless and impractical, causing you to make the same mistake over and over again. People think you are stupid.

Pisces (Feb.19 - Mar.20) - You have a vivid imagination and often think you are being followed by the CIA or FBI. You have minor influence over your associates, and people resent you for flaunting it at your peers. You lack confidence and are generally a coward. Pisces people do horrible things to small animals.

Aries (Mar. 21 - Apr.19) - You are the pioneer type and hold most people in contempt. You are quick-tempered, impatient, and scornful of advice. You are not very nice.

Taurus (Apr.20 - May 20) - You are impractical and persistent. You have a dogged determination and work like hell. Most people think you are stubborn and bull-headed. You are a communist.

Gemini (May 21 - June 20) - You are quick and an intelligent thinker. People like you because you are bisexual. However, you are inclined to expect too much for too little. This means you are cheap. Gemini's are known for committing incest.

Cancer (June 21 - July 22) - You are sympathetic and understanding to other people's problems. They think you are a sucker. You are always putting things off. That's why you'll never make anything of yourself. Most welfare recipients are Cancer people.

Leo (July 23 - August 22) - You consider yourself a born leader. Others think you are pushy. Most Leo people are bullies. You are vain and dislike honest people. Your arrogance is disgusting. Leo people are known thieves. Mr. Goolsby is a Leo.

Virgo (Aug.23 - Sept.22) - You are the logical type and hate disorder. This nit-picking is sickening to your friends. You are cold and unemotional and sometimes fall asleep during love-making. Virgos make good bus drivers.

Libra (Sept.23 - Oct.22) - You are the artistic type and have a difficult time with reality. If you are a man, you more than likely are gay. Chances for employment and monetary gains are excellent. Most Libra women are good ladies of the evening. Many Libra people die of Herpes Simplex 2.

Scorpio (Oct.23- Nov.21) - You are shrewd in business and cannot be trusted. You shall achieve the pinnacle of success because of your total lack of ethics. Most Scorpio people are murdered.

Sagittarius (Nov.22 - Dec.21) - You are optimistic and enthusiastic. You have a reckless tendency to rely on luck since you lack talent. The majority of Sagittarians are drunks or dope addicts. People laugh at you a great deal.

Capricorn (Dec.22 - Jan. 19) - You are conservative and afraid of taking risks. You don't do much of anything and are lazy. There has never been a Capricorn of any importance. Capricorn should avoid standing still too long, as they tend to take root and become trees.

Most of all, beware those born on a cusp...

Chapter 12
Promoting Management People

Promoting management people is different than selecting management people, because you will have had a chance to observe the person being considered for promotion firsthand. You will have judged her tenacity. In the selection process, you can discern something about a person's intelligence from their school class rank. In the small business environment, you can pass judgment on a person's tenacity, and tenacity will win out over intelligence, particularly in business.

My brother-in-law frequently tells the story of his roommate in medical school who had to wait a year for admission because of his low entrance exam score. However, he came from a family of doctors, and even though of only average intelligence, he graduated first in his class. He wanted success more than many of those superior to him in intelligence. How fortunate that the Creator made it possible for ones such as he to overcome by desire what they lack in brains - to achieve success simply by willing it so.

Marginal IQ's are estimated to be 105 according to *The Book of Lists*. Two examples of the importance of motivation over average intelligence are the famous Spanish author Cervantes, who authored the classic, *Don Quixote*, and Copernicus, the Polish founder of modern astronomy, who put forth the radical (for its time) theory that the earth and other planets revolved around the sun.

Don't be trapped into confusing tenacity with hard work. The notion that hard work inevitably leads to success is sheer nonsense. If the manager you are considering for promotion is success-oriented, he will keep his eye on a moving target. He is interested in results, not doctrines. He will learn the game you are playing and how your company keeps score. He will ask himself the questions, "What business am I in?", and, "What does it take to be successful in this business?" It is not enough to simply "produce" in a job. You must convince others of your proficiency. *You must promote yourself.*

It's the same as learning how to study, which simply means that you must establish priorities and filter out those which are not important. You must be intent on learning what your teacher deems important.

In short, the promotable person in small business must have, like the owner, desire, persistence, and guts, and must be able to keep his sights focused on what is important.

When you face the task of choosing between two competing candidates for a job promotion, give attention to the personal lifestyles of each. The person who can't balance their checkbook or cope with their family could become a really big problem for you.

Some people think that one way to judge a person is to test their mettle on the golf course or a tennis court, or hand ball court.

Tennis Courts

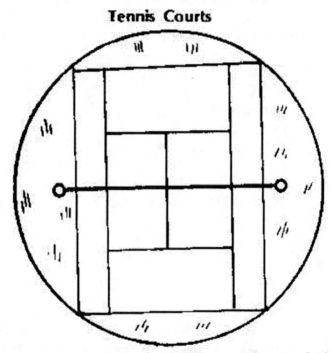

For small business executive with a well rounded game

Others think you can learn a lot about a person by the way they perform at the bridge table, or in a poker game. Watching a person's attitude in sports will give you much insight into their business aptitude. All of us have seen the golfer who refuses to play a short, safe shot to a water hazard and then cross it with another shot,

91

thinking a perfectly hit two wood - which isn't in their repertoire - would be a better attack, or, a tennis player who constantly attempts to hit low-percentage down-the-alley shots when a cross-court would win more points.

Bridge can shed insight on the manager's business judgment. Playing infrequently and with different partners, there is a need to use your inborn common sense, which happens to be what you are looking for when promoting a manager.

If the candidates for promotion are not card players, you might just ask for solutions to these fun problems selected from IQ tests:

1. It is ten miles to the airport. To make your plane, you must average 60 miles per hour. En route, you run into traffic and only average 30 mph for the first five miles. What must you average the rest of the way to make your plane?

2. If a train a mile long is approaching a mile-long tunnel at 60 mph, how long will it take for the train to get through the tunnel?

3. What number logically completes this series: 7, 12, 27, 72, 207, ---.

4. There is a rule of arithmetic that applies across and down. Find the rule and figure out the missing number:

6	2	4
2	?	0
4	0	4

5. Complete the analogy by writing a word in the space, ending with the letter printed: High is to low as sky is to: - - - -H.

6. Complete the following analogy: C, G, Q are to F, V, R as T, X, H are to (1) V, L. G. (2) B, F, Y (3) W, M, I (4) N, Z, D, (5) A, B, C.

Answers:
    1. You missed the plane already
    2. Two minutes
    3. 612
    4. The missing number is 2
    5. Earth
    6. C. G. Q are to F, V, R as T, X, H are to W, M, I

If you'd rather not administer a formal written test which, after all, cannot measure the all important traits of grit and tenacity, you might try the Dewars Scotch name test. After chug-a-lugging a fifth of Dewars Scotch, the manager who can correctly guess their own name is given the promotion. (Reference DEWAR'S profile on page vi).

Occasionally, tests or other endeavors need not be considered. There are those odd employees that think they have what "it" takes to be a "C-level" executive. However, when you come across the following scratch pad in a manager's desk, you first wonder how he or she got to where they are. Then, you come to your senses and know what you must do. Hire the other manager and send *this* person to the unemployment line, or, better still, put them in a nice white jacket and have them committed to a place with a very high fence:

Chapter 13
Avoiding Card Carriers

From the standpoint of business history, the twentieth century can be divided into three parts: The first third was dominated by management; the middle third was owned by labor; and the last third was dominated by the consumer.

No one can doubt the suppression of the working class during the first third of the century – caused, in part, by an oversupply of labor. The original useful purpose served by the labor movement has long since passed, and now labor is an archconservative, lethargic bureaucracy that resists the constructive change and progress produced by quality management. Labor unions are a thorn in the flesh, particularly the flesh of the small businessmen. Some wounds have been known to become infectious, producing lockjaw and sometimes death. *All* such wounds leave permanent, unsightly scars.

The Taft-Hartley Act of 1947 brought a balance of power to union and management relations. To keep a union out of your small business, remember:

1. The phone number of the best labor lawyer in your area.
2. Call your labor lawyer at the first sign of any union activity. If you are a poor listener, it is possible that the first time you become aware that a union campaign has been conducted is when a union organizer attempts to show you how many signed union-authorization cards he has. If you allow this you could get a union without an election. Call the first moment you are aware of any union activity, not after you play Go Fishing with an organizer using a deck of union authorization cards.
3. It is completely legal to tell your employees how you feel about a union. The following words are to be remembered and should appear in writing on the employee bulletin board and handbook. "Our overall pay and benefit program is one of the best in this area. It reflects our company's ability and desire to compensate you fairly and our long-established policy of equity of all. We have an outstanding record of progress, and we are proud of our history of

sharing our success with those who have made it possible - you, our employees. Our continued progress depends on a relationship of mutual respect and trust. This relationship, so essential to the future of all of us, has thrived because it is based on the principle of the individual employee's right to deal directly with management. We believe that this relationship can endure only so long as the company and its employees can work directly and personally with each other without outside interference. We have never had a labor union of any sort at this company, and it is the company's sincere belief that one will never be needed. No employee here has ever had to pay dues, fines, initiation fees or assessments to a union, or participate in a strike in order to get fair treatment. No labor union was needed to obtain the high level of benefits and pay and excellent working conditions we have. We want to continue to deal directly with you and your fellow employees in the future as we have in the past. We believe that this is the best way to ensure progress and prosperity for everyone.

Tell this to new employees during orientation. Continue to preach this good news to all your people. Then tell it to the mountains.

Remember to practice the art of making a union unnecessary by continually auditing your performance in these key employee relation areas: communications, ethics, administration of discipline, suggestions and complaints, job content, growth opportunities, performance appraisal and recognition, compensation and benefits, working conditions, personnel administration, and quality of supervisions. No lip service. Deeds! One unwarranted firing in front of others, for example, can render null and void countless platitudes of company fairness and even possibly undermine the effectiveness of "attaboy".

If you and your management team subscribe to and sincerely practice leadership by example, you will *never* have a union. You can count on it! Denying yourself the perquisites visible to all employees - limousines, lavish offices, private secretaries, parking places, and management dining rooms, free office coffee machines, company vacation villas - will destroy the barriers frequently erected between management and labor.

A Spartan management will never need to post a notice like this one:

Notice

Management regrets that it has come to their attention that new, card-carrying employees dying on the job are failing to fall down.

This practice must stop!

It has become impossible to distinguish between death and the natural movement of our workforce. Therefore, any union employees found dead while in an upright position **will be terminated !!!!!!!**

In all fairness, there is one defense of unions that needs to be stated and at the same time gives me the opportunity to editorialize. Politicians and the public love to denounce inflation and pin the blame on unions even more than on big businesses. Well, this just won't wash. The cause of inflation is our government. And it is easy to overlook, considering all the rhetoric and the naming of scapegoats, such as unions. When all the layers of onionskin are peeled back, our government is exposed as the cause of inflation. How does our government cause such inflation? Oversupply of money and budget deficits.

$335,000,000,000

CBO's Projected Net Budget Deficit 2007
"A million here, a million there, pretty soon it starts to add up to real money". Everette Dirksen

More precisely, it is the budget deficits now running at approximately $335 billion per year! Not even the all-powerful Federal Reserve Board, headed by Bush appointee Ben Bernanke, with its ability to choke off the money supply, can scotch the ever-spiraling inflation rate, at least not without a lot of help from Washington.

What other ways does our government cause inflation? Maybe we should make a partial listing and start with the large percent of the federal budget which goes to pay interest on the national debt. Also, Congress persists in voting itself rather healthy pay hikes in addition to healthy increases for federal workers. This would not concern me if federal workers were as productive as those in the private sector. In a recent survey, it was revealed that federal supervisors would fire more than one-third of their government workers for lack of performance if present firing restrictions for federal workers were not so stringent.

Social Security taxes certainly contribute to inflation. And, understand the company will have to equally match the employee contribution.

Energy taxes and farm supports are costs to be borne, ultimately, by all consumers. Also, the automatic escalation which is built into just about all federal and military pensions, wage contracts, food stamps, most state and local pay, social security, and welfare programs contributes to inflation.

Certainly there is nothing wrong with protecting against income erosion, but it does have to be paid for. Of course, we know who does the paying, don't we?

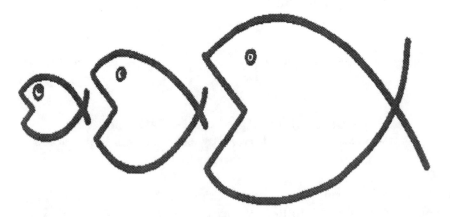

There is no free lunch!

Government regulations and paper work, which load extra work onto companies by the ton, is a huge expense and a contributor to government-ignited inflation. It accounts for a cost of over $18 billion annually to small businesses alone. To briefly touch on this cost to big businesses, I cite one compelling 'fer instance - F. I. DuPont de Nemours & Co., spends $5 million and 180 man-years of work annually to file 15,000 reports to the federal government.

Also, repeated, albeit relatively small, increases in the minimum wage certainly hook into, and pull up, the cost of living in this country. When you hear people say that unions are the big cause of inflation, you will recognize it as an old wives' tale. If we have the high seven-come-eleven inflation rates in the future, you need only wait and watch the inevitable telltale circling of vultures to lead them to the victim's carcass. Paradoxically, perhaps the solution should be to slap wage and price controls on government!

Chapter 14
With 'Gold Stars and Attaboys'

Generalizing, one can almost say tardiness is a management problem, and absenteeism is a labor problem.

Executive's excuse for tardiness: Cigarette caught in the door of an elevator chock full of folks...

Management should operate by Lombarde time, which means turning the clock's big hand ahead 15 minutes. Only Congress is allowed to touch the fat, little hand as it wishy-washes from standard to daylight-saving time. This is to set an example for the people and to organize work assignments in advance, so work can begin immediately when employees arrive. The floor manager of a department store, for example, wants to have his assignments prepared for the beginning of the work shift.

Also, after a break or meal time, the floor manager wants to be in the work area, knowing that starting work is often harder than work itself. Not only can lost man-hours at the beginning of a work cycle be minimized, but the demeaning punch clock could become as obsolete as the yellow-dog contract.

Color me yellow

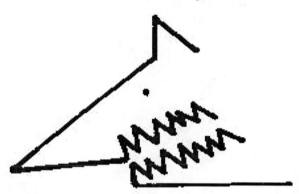

Except during the beginning and the end of the work periods, management's presence is not necessary if assignments have been properly made.

Costly absenteeism can best be minimized through proper hiring, but immediate improvement can be accomplished if management places emphasis on absenteeism. For example, when a worker, who has been absent, returns to work, his supervisor should have an informal session with him, explaining that his presence was missed and emphasizing the importance of attendance - all done diplomatically, of course.

Having learned in child psychology to ignore disobedience and lack of cooperation, and to strongly reward constructive behavior, such as employee attendance, you might reward the employee who has a good record of attendance without tardiness.

Both tardiness and absenteeism are indications of job dissatisfaction. By studying the employee's attendance and lateness record, barring a major medical problem, when the employee will quit can almost be predicted to the day. On the other hand, an improving trend on the person's attendance record shows increased job satisfaction.

There is at least one school of medical thinking which links a person's health to his job satisfaction and happiness. Job dissatisfaction causes mental anxiety, which leads to poor health. Regardless of cause and effect, you will find attendance records helpful in pinpointing job dissatisfaction, predicting quits, and avoiding costly down time.

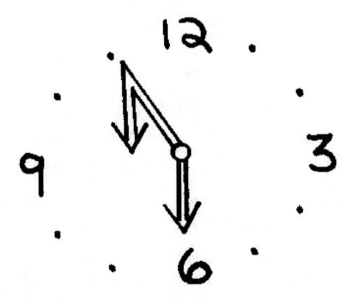

When you hear a manager complain, "I have given my people everything, including good pay which is the highest in these parts, incentive plans paying big money for production, generous fringe benefits and yet they are dissatisfied," you know you have a manager who does not understand that people work more for job satisfaction than for wages or salaries. Pasting a gold star on an employee's forehead can go a long way in germinating the seeds of job satisfaction.

Until A. H. Maslow's attitude surveys proved that good wages frequently took third or fourth place behind "challenging work," "job satisfaction" and other non-wage considerations, it was generally assumed that people worked to satisfy material needs. Good pay was assumed to be the greater incentive. Today, employees want to satisfy their souls along with their material needs.

By charisma and personal relationship between management and employees, a small business can hold its wages and salaries - all other things being equal below larger, more impersonal businesses. Employees are willing to forego additional compensation if they are stroked with meaningful "attaboy"!

This wage and salary differential can be found among a few large businesses, where the major company concentrates more on insuring job satisfaction but is more common in small businesses because of the workers' access to the ownership people and connection to a dream, especially if the service or product helps others.

CERTIFICATE

**FOR YOUR VERY OUTSTANDING PERFORMANCE
YOU ARE AWARDED**

"ONE ATTABOY"

One thousand 'ATTABOYS' qualifies you to be Leader of Men,
to Work Overtime with a Smile, Explain assorted Problems to
Management, and be looked upon as a Local Hero
— Without a raise in Pay.

Awarded this Date

by _____

The desire to benefit mankind is near universal. Successful entrepreneurs teach this daily and weave this value into the company's fabric. A rather amusing example of a major company's chief executive failing to award "attaboys" was provided by Henry Singleton of Teledyne. The *Wall Street Journal* reports of a meeting where a subsidiary head praised a subordinate for dramatically increasing cash flow. The subsidiary head then turned to the boss, Mr. Singleton, asking if the subordinate's performance didn't merit his congratulations, too. Singleton coolly replied, "The fact that I didn't comment otherwise should be congratulations enough." In this same situation, a small business "attaboy" giver would have awarded an iron cross for meritorious performance on the spot, knowing this symbolic stroking to be worth more than additional salary.

It is common knowledge that the owner typically gives off more feeling for the business than the large business technocrat. You can create local heroes out of your employees with "attaboys" without additional pay, provided the sincerity is manifest. You can keep your wage rate below your larger competitors. You can keep your productivity above them.

In conclusion, it is not sufficiently appreciated, even at the board level, the importance of all employees fully understanding and buying into the company's mission and values. Moreover, it is enormously important that leadership weaves into the company's culture and employees the value of the product or service to the customer and how each employee can help mankind. Helping our fellowman is a core human desire. The employee satisfaction of helping others is substantially under-addressed in business practice and literature. When such understanding permeates throughout, attitude and productivity will meaningfully improve and, in the aggregate, impact our gross national output.

Chapter 15
Death is No Excuse

On each employee's anniversary date with the company, the small business owner should visit the employee at his work station to let him know how much he is appreciated and to remind him of the importance of experienced personnel with years of service in the company. Such a visit creates the proper atmosphere - to thank the employee, and impress upon him the importance of seniority – and, it provides opportunity for feedback to management. The very important employee feedback will usually flow quite naturally at this time. A simple, "How do you like it here?" can elicit the desired feedback if need be. It requires a small expenditure of your time but will return its weight in gold.

If you have any doubt about the worker's belief in the importance of his job, preface your remarks with something like, "I know you are extremely busy, and I will interrupt you only for a moment..." Be assured, employees on the production line or shipping department will acknowledge that his time is indeed very valuable, but he will appreciate your visit, and it will help him to cast a kindly and more sympathetic eye toward management. Many management people who did not come up through the ranks and believe that "all my employees care about is pay and quitting time" are quite shocked to find this employee involvement.

Employee relations can be strengthened by recognizing employees on the company welcoming marquee, which should be mounted at the visitors' entrance to the business. Don't confuse the welcoming marquee with the employees' bulletin board. Even though you mainly use the welcoming marquee to place visitors' names, such as customers, vendors and outside consultants, and also for a new product headlines, the marquee, in conjunction with the employee bulletin board, will give special recognition to the worker whose 15-year anniversary is at hand, or, to the one who has just been named a director of the Rotary Club.

In the work area, out of public view, a high-quality, lighted, glass encased employee bulletin board should be mounted in a place accessible to all employees. This will be your primary method of written communication with your employees, even in the new internet world with its daily avalanche of e-mails.

The substance of a formal communication to all employees should be prepared and reviewed in a most judicious manner. The form of the formal communication should receive as much consideration as its substance to get the employees to bother to read it and then to receive the communication with enthusiasm.

Rather than simply typing the message on company stationery and sticking it on an unlighted, inaccessible board, try these suggestions to get attention and readership: Put items of common interest - light news events, such as a story of Kobe Bryant scoring a hole-in-one - on the board. In addition to current events, include news items about employees themselves with a heavy dose of snapshots of the honored employees similar to what you'd want to see in a company newsletter.

Your formal company communications here can be spruced up by printing your company name in giant size type or by dressing it up with a neat colored border made of construction paper. You might have the communication written by a calligrapher, or try longhand in white ink on black paper, perhaps with a sketch of a flower on the border, or any other doodle to attract attention. A telegram authored and posted by management, for example, is an excellent attention-getter. The message here is simply to avoid the conventional, boring letter.

The reason for the board being under glass is not to preserve the pheasant but to prevent alterations to communications. It is a simple thing for a wag to scratch out the word "not" in this communiqué:

"Employees attending the company awards banquet Saturday night will *[not]* be required to wear formal dress."

What an embarrassment to you, if you plan to wear a sport jacket and high-top tennis shoes and your companion for the evening appears in a cocktail dress! Too, encasing the bulletin board will prevent the appearance of such employee-inspired pranks as this:

Sickness: No excuse. We will no longer accept your doctor's statement as proof since we believe that if you are able to go to the doctor, you are able to come to work.

Death: (Other than your own): This is no excuse. There is nothing you can do for them, and we are sure that someone else in a lesser position can attend to the arrangements. However, if the funeral can be held in late afternoon, we will be glad to let you off one hour early provided that your share of work is ahead enough to keep the job going in your absence.

Death: (Your own) This will be accepted as an excuse, but we would like a two-week notice since we feel it is your duty to teach someone else your job. Don't let us down on this one, or, as Mark Twain said, the announcement of your death will be greatly exaggerated.

Leave of Absence: (For an operation) We are no longer allowing this practice. We wish to discourage any thoughts you may be having about needing an operation. We believe that as long as you are employed here, you will need all of whatever you have and should not consider having anything removed. We hired you as you are, and to have anything removed would certainly make you less than we bargained for.

Restroom: Too much time is being spent in the Restroom. In the future, we will follow the practice of going to the Restroom in alphabetical order. For instance, those whose names begin with "A" will go from 8 a.m. to 8:05a.m., "B" will go from 8:05 a.m. to 8: 10 a.m., and so on. If you are unable to go at your appointed time, it will be necessary to wait until the next day when your turn comes again. Ouch…

The shortcoming of the bulletin board is that it does not allow the valuable feedback offered in the anniversary section with the worker at his station. There is no reason you can't employ both.

Honest feedback is critical. The lunchroom is an excellent place to get feedback as well as break down the unwanted barrier of management "rank". Bring your brown bag and thermos bottle occasionally, and eat with your people. Make certain you do not initiate shop talk - let the employees do that - but never, never discourage it.

You would not want to make a decision purely on the basis of employee feedback for the sake of the chain of command, if for no other reason. Be forewarned, the first three or four lunches in the employee lunch area will be awkward both for you and for the employees. It may never become a fun activity for you, but the enormity of the feedback and the chance to establish friendships will make the visits worthwhile.

Like to meet people? Like a change? Like excitement?
Like a new job? Just screw up one more time...

Audiovisual Presentation to Publicize Your Message

The use of a slide presentation with narration is a powerful way to communicate with your people. The subject matter can range from quality control to your retirement plan to new service or product methods. Be sure to include slides of the very people you are addressing, where possible, for maximum impact. Levity, especially poking fun at management, is well received. Don't overlook crossing slide presentations between two separate functions in the same company. For example, purchasing can greatly benefit by seeing matters concerning retail sales - even if it is only a sales training film. It gives each department or division a better overview and another piece of the overall picture puzzle can be laid into place. Unlike the army practice of keeping the troops from knowing the objectives of and reasons for their mission, total communication which necessitates openness is a must for success in business, large or small. PowerPoint™ and slide presentations are very inexpensive in addition to being an outstanding way to communicate and provide an excellent opportunity to emphasize once again the company's mission and values and how employee's daily work benefits their fellow man.

If you have a message to bring to the attention of many people in diverse places, a slide presentation with pre-recorded narration to fit each slide may be your way to create something like the masterpiece movie adaptation of *Occurrence at Owl Creek Bridge* on a small budget.

The audience for your message will be commercially oriented. They will be a captive audience, and, if you're lucky, your message will have a lingering effect. It is a fine idea, but before going further, let's make mention of some other commonly used systems for getting messages across to large groups of people.

Perhaps they begin with mere written reports, directed to the people whom you wish to reach. Another method is a simple slide presentation with still photos projected on a screen in a logical order. A commentator talks about each slide while changing the slides. No amplified recording with a professional voice is used.

Another method is to use large flip charts, with each message prominently set forth, perhaps with some artwork. Again, a commentator explains the meaning of each flip page. More sophisticated methods may involve the installation of overhead projectors or interphone communication via teleconferencing. Chalk boards, brochures, PowerPoint, and even movies are not uncommon. In today's computer age, communications grow ever more sophisticated. The possibilities are endless.

However, communications methods must fit your budget. Big companies can sometimes afford to squander money, but small companies cannot.

Use a digital camera equipped with multi-exposure and video still capability to take your photos. Then, put photos to an audio voiceover by someone with a good speaking voice, a voice the listener does not hear every day. If Orson Welles is unavailable, you might consider your minister. If to be shown outside the company, consider hiring a local radio commentator to read or record the narrative you prepare. The human voice remains the most powerful means of communication.

You will then deliver your presentation. Turn it into a slide show or Powerpoint. By using your personal camera, you can literally set up shop for very little cost. Slides with audio can be extremely effective when well-choreographed and is a major reason for recommending this little used technique.

While you were engaged in formal education training, you learned both by reading and by listening. The audiovisual approach is nothing more than an adaptation of the basic principles you first experienced during school years. It still works.

Unlike a commercial movie, which also combines the processes of seeing and hearing, the slides with audio can be continuously updated. A just-completed movie is almost immediately obsolete in the rapidly changing business world, but a slide presentation, by virtue of its versatility, is substantially superior to a movie presentation unless, of course, you pour enough money into film production to produce a blockbuster.

Words seem to be better received with a still, rather than a moving picture, and help to improve the listener's retention. This is certainly true when the slide is of a graph, map or financial figures, all common business subjects. The old opaque or transparent overhead projector, in contrast, was much inferior due, in part, to the speaker himself and the distraction of fumbling with materials.

The idea of an audio-slide presentation with a clear third-party voice, secure both from interruption and long-winded asides, adds more objectivity and authenticity to the presentation, considerably more than the boss' or salesman's voice which, on occasion, induces sleep. You might also find the buyer wanting all his people to hear the presentation, in which case you will find yourself with a captive audience.

Music can easily be introduced as a background for the commentator to set the mood. Other background sound effects such as lighting, children's voices, the sound of factory machinery operating, even a Huntley-Brinkley act, can be added as dramatics. If you let your in-house talent produce these dramatics rather than your ad agency, so much the better.

Here, now, are some examples of how simple, easy to produce, low-cost slide audio presentations can be used:

1. New product or service presentations to customers, company directors, or financial investors.
2. A financial presentation to the company audit committee, or commercial or investment banker.
3. Company training and/or motivational sessions.
4. Special seminars for production people.
5. Retail floor training sessions.
6. Monthly company meetings.

Yes, the combination of voiceover accompanying still slides is pretty hard to beat. And it's available to firms with even austere budgets. Try it. The results produced will be impressive.

If your company grows to 150 or more employees, you may begin to lose the personal touch. You may want to consider sponsoring a thirty-minute commercial radio music program, jockeyed by a well-known and likeable management person, preferably the personnel officer, if he or she is capable. This can be a valuable tool to prevent employee turnover in a tight labor market and attract new employees.

It is recommended that the program be aired during the half hour just after quitting time. The program is especially effective in small communities and can be good company and product advertisement as well. This, of course, does not replace the conventional ways to strengthen employee relations, such as, press releases recognizing employee accomplishments. A thirty-minute monthly radio show should carry news items about employees. Use the program to extol employee work performances: a particular employee adjusted a record twenty-one insurance claims during the week.

Here is one other possibility: mount a large employee retirement/death plaque, preferably in bronze, in a conspicuous place. Upon death, upon retirement, or even while still working, the employee's name should be engraved on the plaque, upon which would be emblazoned an appropriate caption: "For loyal service to Lotta Moving and Storage Company." List employee names in order of death, retirement or accomplishment without regard to rank while employed. Immortality is desired by most, and the bronze plaque is a lot closer to this desire than a round of coffee on the day of retirement or a slap on the back for a job well done. It is also more meaningful than the traditional gold watch and much less expensive.

One might remember that those who continue to be employed take their cue on the way the company feels about retirees from the way retirees are treated on return visits and in pension checks much more than from the giving of retirement mementos. Retirees are an under-served asset where small investments can yield large benefits.

Some All-Purpose Rubber Stamps and Routing Slips

It is not true to say that Washington has been no help to the small businessman. The rubber stamps used so effectively there have also been of much benefit to the small businessman. It is beneficial to the small company. Stamps are a gentle and quick way to send a message without being personal or wordy.

Three rubber stamps are recommended, although you may identify a need for additional stamps for your small business and management personalities. Here they are:

One stamp fits any business, and all personalities: KAPOK, which literally means the stuffing for lifejackets. KAPOK is the classic euphemism:

By courtesy of Halderman, Erlichmann and the Third Reich in their covert activities, this next stamp provides a catchy way of rubber stamping a document, letter, envelope or memo as very "Strictly Confidential/Private":

EYES ONLY

The next stamp (one of my personal favorites...) means "This is unimportant. Please route to a clerical staff member for disposition." In more blunt language, it means, "I don't want you to spend your $25-per-hour management time on a $5 per hour job."

WHATEVER

Routing slips with appropriate boxes to check provide an additional way to communicate, particularly with subordinates, using few words. Many managers have trouble coping with the problem of dismissing a manager. Others have problems passing on this bad news without feeling compelled to gush forth reasons, which can get you a fat lawsuit if any of the accusations are false. Consider using the routing slip on the next page, and simply check off your preferences. This routing slip can solve both the problem of timidity and talking too much, not to mention its strict adherence to the principles of political correctness:

Onassis Chemical Supply Company

To: _____

From: _____

Date: _____

_____ See company policy statement on page 31 of *Joy of Cooking.*

_____ For your information.

_____ I need the sordid skinny on Mrs. /Ms. /Mr. _____, the new good-looker in the Department. Please take charge of this.

_____ Can we discuss further tire rotation on your station wagon?

_____ Attach the top part of this form to your forehead with heavy duty staple gun.

_____ How would you like a flat lip, fella?

_____ For your signature. Just your last name, Dummy.

_____ Could you put a stop to the heavy panting and moaning drifting out of the lounge?

_____ Could you clarify office position on starched shirts with French cuffs?

_____ Hmm. A talking turkey who plays an oboe? Better re-check your sources.

_____ You are laid-off.

_____ You are fired.

_____ You are fired, your desk has been turned over, your office has been locked, your files have been confiscated, and this month's paycheck has been canceled. Moreover, we cannot recommend you to future prospective employers. By the way, I take great pleasure in this action.

Remarks: (Please use space below for comments. We do not guarantee they will be read...)

Ok. That's enough space...

Chapter 16
How to Find a B.C.

Like speaking in public, business letters convey an image of your business by the form as well as the substance of the letters. (E-mail will never be a suitable replacement for them.) Your company stationery should be on high quality paper, engraved with your company name and embossed with your corporate logo. Avoid using company colors - something of a fad of late. Many companies are wisely discouraging company stationery printed with individual names and titles because of cost and the vanity factor (Not to mention that a top management purge would leave behind some pretty expensive scratch paper...). The highest quality, white stationery is the most acceptable. It produces the cleanest letter and certainly conveys authority. Don't overlook the style of software fonts. Keep it neat and bold. A scruffy letter can make the most important business letter go unanswered.

In signing your letter, use a pen with black ink. Felt-tipped and ballpoint pens are clerical, not management, tools.

As to the ever increasing cost of mail, I know only one sure way to beat the post office. Put your own name and address in the middle of the envelope where the name and address of the person you're sending the letter to would normally go. In the upper left-hand corner, put the other person's name and address - and don't put a stamp on it. Then, put the letter in the mailbox. Right away the post office sees no stamp - who do they send it to? You guessed it! The person listed in the left-hand corner.

Compilation of a form letter book, with certain no-brainer recurring letters filed by numbers, is a definite time saver. Attempt to keep your form letters from reading like a laundry list. Here is an example of a form-type letter in which the sender congratulates the receiver on an honor they received. Of course, editing in some instances is appropriate to personalize the message, as was done in the last paragraph here:

MEX FIREARMS, INC

February 22, 1836

Colonel W. B. Travis
San Antonio, Texas

Dear Colonel Travis:

I was delighted to learn from a recent news account that you have been elected Chairman of the Board of Trustees of The Alamo. I fully realize that it is something you undertake with mixed feelings. However, I know the importance of this position, the positive contribution to the community it entails, and that your selection reflects the high regard and confidence in which you are held by your colleagues. I extend my warmest congratulations on your appointment and the obviously successful career which preceded it.

Hope to see you, Bowie and Crockett in the very near future.

Sincerely yours,

Antonio Lopez De Santa Anna
President

Since we've gone to such lengths to make stationery our strongest advertising piece, inspection at random of the envelopes and the proper addresses, as well as the neatness of inserting the letter in the envelope, and making sure the letter is being sent to the right party, are suggested. By inspection, you will avoid the embarrassment of a mail clerk inadvertently sending a price quotation letter intended for a prospective customer to an existing customer and revealing to him a quote lower than what he paid.

You may also avoid the type of embarrassment recently experienced by a New York detective agency which had been hired to shadow a faithless husband. The wronged wife complained that the agency had sent the surveillance report to her husband and the bill to her! Not good...

12 E-mail Don'ts

We are all receiving a tsunami of electronic words. You want your e-mails to stand out and achieve results in the middle of this tidal wave of print. This is so important that rather than the enlightened way of changing behavior by positive reinforcement, we need to get your full attention with a list of, "Don't do this, Dummy!" Pay attention.

1. *Don't* forget etiquette. E-mails require gentility as a show of respect for the recipient. Just because the person is not standing in front of you and just because there is not an exchange of spoken words, don't presume etiquette is not necessary.
2. *Don't* just start into the subject of the e-mail. Begin with "Dear Jane:" even if the message is one line: "I will be glad to have a two martini power lunch with you and then initiate a hostile tender offer for Boeing." End all e-mails with a programmed closing such as, "With best personal regards, Sincerely, John", or appropriately spaced similar formal closing. This can be inserted in each e-mail by clicking your signature icon.
3. *Don't* use all lower case or ALL UPPERCASE IN YOUR E-MAILS.
4. *Don't* overuse exclamation marks!!!!!!!!!!!!!!! One is sufficient.
5. *Don't* write longer than 2 paragraphs. If longer, use an attachment for backup and details, or, pick up the phone and call instead.
6. *Don't* disregard the importance of the subject line which should summarize the message contained in the body in one brief sentence.
7. *Don't* ever presume you are anonymous using e-mail. 'Cause you ain't.
8. *Don't* send an emotionally charged e-mail when you are angry. Either wait 24 hours, or type it and push it up into your draft folder to be reconsidered the next day after your motor's cooled down.
9. *Don't* send the e-mail to the wrong person. It's Murphy's Law that this is more likely to happen when you have mentioned a person's name in the body in a negative way. And the next thing

you know you have put that persons name in "Send". Don't be so frisky.

10. Speaking of friskiness, *don't* click "Send" until you have edited your own message. You can avoid misspellings with spell check. However, you need to check for wrong verb tenses, missing words, misused words (such as amphibious when you really mean ambidextrous) and the many homonyms in our language which successfully hide from a computer spell check. By all means double-check that the attachment referenced is attached. Make it habit to pause after each e-mail and go over this mental check list. I have programmed my e-mails to go into the "outbox" after striking "Send" to force the discipline of this review even on the most minor e-mails. You want the reader to witness literacy. You want the reader to be inclined to respond favorably to your courteous and well written e-mail.

11. *DON'T* commit anything to email that you would be ashamed to see as a lead story in the newspaper, on TV, in the tabloids, in someone else's memoirs, in a book about what not to do when starting a small business and especially as part of a subpoena asking you to produce documents in a court proceeding involving you and your company.

12. Last, but far from least, *DON'T* assume that when you hit the "Delete" key your e-mail is erased for all time. It isn't! When information can be recovered from smashed black boxes and shattered hard drives, certainly your e-mail is recoverable by computer experts and hackers employed by intelligence agencies to ferret out information floating out there in cyberspace.

Beware! If you don't want it to be seen, don't commit it to the Internet. Just as surely as your DNA identifies you almost beyond reasonable doubt, your e-mail, once committed to the Web, does so with 100% accuracy and may as well be stamped across your forehead. The Biblical admonition applies: Surely your sin will find you out!

If you must convey confidential information do it the old-fashioned way. Write it down, let it be read, and then eat it if you must. Most paper is digestible. I guarantee your time on the witness stand with a piece of incriminating e-mail in the hands of a prosecuting attorney won't suit your palette nearly as much. This warning will self-destruct in five seconds.

Cell Phone Civility

Create a two-arms length distance from others when speaking on your cell phone

When you are in apublic location and cannot create private space, acknowledge people nearby with an "Excuse Me."

Before going into a meeting, make sure your cell phone is turned off.

Make a note that when your cell phone is on vibrate, the sound is still considered "noise pollution" to others.

Business Letter and Report Writing

Our educational system has deteriorated. Social promotions, grade inflation and declining SAT scores are but a few manifestations of the lack of emphasis on the blocking and tackling of education, the three Rs. If I sound like Chicken Little, know that the problem is acute enough to be recognized by bootblacks.

A PhD planted after one's name is no guarantee that the possessor can write clearly. Sometimes the more educated, the more likely it is that he or she will be unable to transmit their thoughts accurately. Moreover, many good business speakers cannot write one paragraph that makes sense to anyone, including Mr. Goolsby.

Information, clear and concise, is essential to a good decision in business. How many times have you seen an otherwise quality decision made on erroneous information with the result being a tragic and needless loss of money and dislocation of people and other resources? (In business gamesmanship you should be well on your way to another department, division or new job before it becomes obvious a bad decision on a major matter has been made, whatever the reason.)

In addition to business letter and report writing containing errors and misleading information, the lack of clarity and conciseness adds to the time to produce and the time to read. The boss and others in the corporate hierarchy resent any wordiness encroaching on their time. The problem is so pervasive as to spawn a mini-industry of writing consultants.

The following authentic letter received by the parents of all pupils at a Houston high school shows not only the lack of clarity and conciseness of writing but the very origin of this problem:

Dear Parent:

Our wonderful school's cross-graded, multi-ethnic, individualized learning program is designed to enhance the concept of an open-ended learning program with emphasis on a continuum of multi-ethnic, academically enriched learning, using the identified intellectually gifted child as the agent or director of his own learning. Major emphasis is on cross-graded, multi-ethnic learning with the main objective being to learn respect for the uniqueness of a person.

Signed,
Principal of a Houston High School.

Huh??? Why not this instead?

Dear Parent:

A program is planned for all students. Students will be encouraged to move at their own speed. Each student will be taught and graded according to his ability to learn.

Kisses and Handstands,
The Principal

cc: Tooth Fairy

These five rules will not make you a good business writer, but can point you in the right direction:

1. Write like you talk. You want the letter to come off just as you would speak. The example on the next page is written in everyday conversational style.

2. Suppress the urge to put down everything you know; include only information germane to the subject at hand. As Sergeant Joe Friday used to say: "Just the facts, ma'am." You may find an outline helpful in this respect. On the other hand, while striving for brevity, don't neglect your main point. Otherwise you may find yourself in the position of the young wife who wrote a letter to her landlord complaining about the lack of a bathroom commode in her newly rented apartment. Afflicted with shyness, she decided to abbreviate "bathroom commode" to B. C., whereupon the landlord, puzzled, assumed that she was inquiring about the location of the nearest Baptist church. By return mail he informed her that a B. C. was located about nine miles from her apartment and was "capable of seating 250 persons."

3. Edit your own writing with the view of deleting phrases which add no substance to your message, such as, "I think you will find" or "As you might remember from my previous correspondence on this subject." Strive to cut the report or letter in half. You will be surprised at your progress. Write legibly.

Dear Ann Landers,
I'm writing to tell you my problem. It seems I have been married to a sex maniac for 12 years. He makes love to me regardless of what I'm doing, ironing, washing dishes, sweeping, etc. I would like to know if there is anything to prevent this? Please excuse this jerky writing. Sincerely
Marilyn

4. Be tactful in your correspondence and write from the reader's viewpoint.
5. In business letters, as in report writing, state your conclusion first unless you can draft a good opening sentence or paragraph showing what's-in-it-for-me to insure reader reception. Consider, for example, the following chain letter:

Dear Friend:
    This letter is sent with the hope of bringing relief and happiness to tired wives.

Unlike most chain letters, this does not cost anything. Simply send a copy of this to five of your married friends who are equally tired. Then bundle your husband and send him to the woman whose name is at the top of the list and add your name to the bottom of it.

When your name comes to the top of the list you will receive 18,437 men and some of them dandies.

Have faith ... don't break this chain. One lady broke the chain and got her old man back.

Sincerely,

A Tired Friend

The business letter is used frequently. Attention to form and substance can be inexpensive, productive advertising. It will convey a positive company image.

Uptown, my child.

Chapter 17
Boffos and Belly Laughs

The way a businessperson uses his or her voice can often determine success. This is true whether the person speaks with individuals or before groups - both important functions in everyday life and each requiring entirely different skills.

Even though speaking engagements can consume a great deal of time and produce unwanted stress, the new small business owner must actively seek (and accept the nomination, if offered) opportunities at civic clubs, trade associations, fraternal organizations, and even church functions. The ability to speak in public, if only to a small group, is a highly desirable and necessary skill for a small business owner. Almost any speaking opportunity should be welcomed, though I'd draw the line at beer garden oratories, unless you are a German.

Two reasons to make speeches are to bring goodwill and recognition to your business and to improve your own ability to communicate in business.

Inasmuch as you will typically be speaking to an audience whose individual time carries a high billing rate (especially if there are plumbers in the audience), you will want to be as effective as possible. You should thoroughly prepare both your subject matter and your delivery. Emphasis should be less on what you say than on how you say it. Herman Melville was fully aware of the importance of delivery in public speaking when he breathed oratory skill into Captain Ahab in the novel *Moby Dick.*

One of the greatest orators of our day is Billy Graham, who speaks with enthusiasm and emphasis, comes straight to the point, and holds firmly to the track. The Graham style was summed up expertly in three paragraphs of a story in *The Charlotte Observe*:

"Graham looks venerable, with his silver sideburns, his sharp nose and a gaze made more formidable by the deep frown wrinkles between his frosty eyebrows. For those who respond with awe to strong male body language, Graham is a magnificent specimen, a Valentino for the Lord."

"The jaw is firm and snaps shut in teeth-grinding seriousness after a biting remark. The face is stern, almost angry. There are no gestures of equivocation, no apologetic mannerisms; the head doesn't tilt in a pleading gesture. There is no squinting, no shoulder-shrugging, no lip puckering, no sweet talk."

"His urgings are more commands than pleadings, and his forceful gestures are effective accompaniment. His index finger chops the air, jabs at his audience. His fists thrust forward..."

Study those paragraphs, and remember the importance of delivery the next time you make a public speech.

To minimize the stress of speaking in public, it may be helpful to recall that great speakers from Mussolini to John Kennedy felt anxious before speaking. According to *The Book of Lists* by Wallace, Wallace and Wallechinsky, the fear of speaking in public is greater still than the fear of death.

The lack of verbal response and the fear of audience rejection are the two basic reasons for stage fright. For the timid among you, both can be overcome with a generous intake of intoxicating spirits. However, your audience may be left scratching their heads as to your subject matter...

Many find that the use of a prop literally moves the spotlight off the speaker and onto the prop, and, of course, enhances audience reception of the message. Be careful in your selection of props, though. A photographer once used a display of pictures as props to illustrate his talk. When he finished, he realized the audience had been so scintillated by the beauty of his scantily clothed models that few had heard a word he said!

What should you do with your hands when speaking? As you know, the unsure travel and detours of your hands can be disconcerting to both the audience and you. Lock your hands on the speaker's rostrum. If there is no speaker's desk, put your hands in your jacket pockets with the thumb of each hand hooked over the top of the pocket. Brian Williams, anchor of the NBC Nightly News broadcast confidently and casually holds a four by ten inch white card in his hands as he speaks. Like Williams, you too can find good ways to still your hands, get them out of your way and appear composed and self-confident.

Always open a talk with a joke unless you're speaking at your best friend's funeral. In choosing a joke suitable for the occasion, gravitate towards brevity. You want to get your audience's immediate attention. A funny story helps you eliminate your fear of speaking in public, and it lets your audience know you are just a regular Joe (or, Josephine...) like their friends.

You should keep in your library a file of business jokes for beginning your speeches. Constantly add fresh material to your repertoire. Here are a few boffos to launch your collection:

The chairman of the board of a large corporation looked around the board room after making his speech in favor of a particular course of action. "Now," he said, "we will take a vote on my recommendations. All opposed, raise your right hand and say, "'I resign."

After a long day, Tarzan returned to the tree house. Jane brought him his usual martini. Tarzan downed it in one gulp, and demanded another. Jane exclaimed, "What's the matter with you?" Tarzan said, "It's a jungle out there."

A surprising number of people think the most important thing in life is money. It's simply not true. Love is the most important thing in life. Personally, I'm quite fortunate because I love money.

Inflation in the country is shocking! Just two years ago an eccentric animal lover died and left his cat $15,000. Today that cat is broke.

A duly licensed physician just out of medical school hung his shingle for the first day of practice. After waiting most of the morning for his first patient, he saw a logging truck stop abruptly in front of his office, and out jumped two lumberjacks carrying a friend whose arm had been caught in a logging machine. Seeing the bloody, mangled arm wrapped in a gunny sack, the new physician exclaimed, "My God, man, we'd better get you to a doctor!"

God's itinerary called for Him to meet with some world leaders. President Bush asked Him during his meeting if there would ever be peace between the U.S. and Russia. God answered, "Yes, but not in your lifetime, Dubya." A subsequent meeting with Putin evoked the question whether there would ever be peace between Russia and China? God replied, "Yes, but not in your lifetime." During his last meeting, Prime Minister Sharron asked God if there would ever be peace between Israel and the Arab nations. God answered, "Yes, but not in my lifetime."

In a television debate during the Senate campaign, Teddy Kennedy's opponent shook his finger at Kennedy, saying, "You have never worked a day in your life," a charge that was obviously true. A few days later, while campaigning in a shoe factory, Kennedy was approached by a burly shoemaker who said he had seen the debate on TV and just wanted Kennedy to know that "you have not missed a damned thing."

A plant foreman was promoted to assistant vice president and received a brand new office. The first morning behind his desk at the head office, a maintenance man knocked on the door and asked to speak to him. The assistant vice president, feeling the urge to impress the young man, picked up his phone and said: "Yes, Senator, thank you, yes. I will pass that along to the Federal Reserve Board this afternoon. Goodbye, sir." Then he turned to the maintenance man with a feeling of superiority saying, "And what do you want?" "Nothing, sir. I just came to hook up your phone."

One fine summer day a big, flashy sedan sporting Texas plates pulled up in front of a Maine farm, a way back from nowhere. "Glad to meet you," said the Texan, spotting the owner sidling towards him. "Nice place you got here. How many acres is it?" "Bout two hundred," came the reply. "Where I come from that's a piddlin' size, if you don't mind my saying so," remarked the Texan. "Why, down home I can drive for most of the morning before I even get to the corner of my ranch." "Ayeh," the Down-easter commiserated, "I had a car like that once, but I got rid of it."

Consider Children's Humor
The following excerpts are actual answers given on history tests and in Sunday school quizzes by children in 5th and 6th grade in Ohio. They were collected over a period of three years by two teachers. Read carefully for grammar, misplaced modifiers, and of course, spelling! Kids should rule the world, as it would be a laugh a minute for us adults and therefore no time to war or argue:

Ancient Egypt was old. It was inhabited by gypsies and mummies who all wrote in hydraulics. They lived in the Sarah Dessert. The climate of the Sarah is so bad that all the inhabitants have to live elsewhere.

Moses led the Hebrew slaves to the Red Sea where they made unleavened bread, which is bread made without any ingredients. Moses went up on Mount Cyanide to get the ten commandos. He died before he ever reached Canada, but his commandos made it.

Solomon had three hundred wives and seven hundred porcupines. He was an actual hysterical figure as well as being in the Bible. It sounds like he was sort of busy too.

The Greeks were a highly sculptured people, and without them we wouldn't have history. The Greeks also had myths. A myth is a young female moth.

Socrates was a famous old Greek teacher who went around giving people advice. They killed him. He later died from an overdose of wedlock which is apparently poisonous. After his death, his career suffered a dramatic decline.

In the first Olympic Games, Greeks ran races, jumped, hurled biscuits, and threw the java. The games were messier then than they show on TV now.

Julius Caesar extinguished himself on the battlefields of Gaul. The Ides of March murdered him because they thought he was going to be made king. Dying, he gasped out, "Same to you, Brutus."

Joan of Arc was burnt to a steak and was canonized by Bernard Shaw for reasons I don't really understand. The English and French still have problems.

Queen Elizabeth was the "Virgin Queen". As a queen she was a success. When she exposed herself before her troops they all shouted "Hurrah!" and that was the end of the fighting for a long while.

It was an age of great inventions and discoveries. Gutenberg invented removable type and the Bible. Another important invention was the circulation of blood.

Sir Walter Raleigh is a historical figure because he invented cigarettes and started smoking.

Sir Francis Drake circumcised the world with a 100 foot clipper, which was very dangerous to all his men.

The greatest writer of the Renaissance was William Shakespeare. He was born in the year 1564, supposedly on his birthday. He never made much money and is famous only because of his plays. He wrote tragedies, comedies, and hysterectomies, all in Islamic pentameter.

Writing at the same time as Shakespeare was Miguel Cervantes. He Wrote Donkey Hote. The next great author was John Milton. Milton wrote Paradise Lost. Since then no one ever found it.

Delegates from the original 13 states formed the Contented Congress. Thomas Jefferson, a Virgin, and Benjamin Franklin were two singers of the Declaration of Independence. Franklin discovered electricity by rubbing two cats backward and also declared, "A horse divided against itself cannot stand." He was a naturalist for sure. Franklin died in 1790 and is still dead.

Abraham Lincoln became America's greatest Precedent. Lincoln's Mother died in infancy, and he was born in a log cabin which he built with his own hands. Abraham Lincoln freed the slaves by signing the Emasculation Proclamation.

On the night of April 14, 1865, Lincoln went to the theater and got shot in his seat by one of the actors in a moving picture show. They believe the assinator was John Wilkes Booth, a supposingly insane actor. This ruined Booth's career.

Johann Bach wrote a great many musical compositions and had a large number of children. In between he practiced on an old spinster which he kept up in his attic. Bach died from 1750 to the present. Bach was the most famous composer in the world and so was Handel. Handel was half German, half Italian, and half English. He was very large.

Beethoven wrote music even though he was deaf. He was so deaf that he wrote loud music and became the father of rock and roll. He took long walks in the forest even when everyone was calling for him. Beethoven expired in 1827 and later died for this.

The nineteenth century was a time of a great many thoughts and inventions. People stopped reproducing by hand and started reproducing by machine. The invention of the steamboat caused a network of rivers to spring up.

Cyrus McCormick invented the McCormick raper, which did the work of a hundred men.

Louis Pasteur discovered a cure for rabbits, but I don't know why.

———————

Charles Darwin was a naturalist. He wrote the Organ of the Species. It was very long people got upset about it and had trials to see if it was really true. He sort of said God's days were not just 24 hours but without watches who knew anyhow? I don't get it.

———————

Madman Curie discovered radio. She was the first woman to do what she did. Other women have become scientists since her, but they didn't get to find radios because they were ready taken.

———————

Karl Marx was one of the Marx Brothers. The other three were in the movies. Karl made speeches and started revolutions. Someone in the family had to have a job, I guess.

———————

Consider Bumper Sticker Sightings
Here is a sampling of profound thoughts to tickle your funny bone:

"The gene pool could use a little chlorine."

"All generalizations are false."

"Change is inevitable, except from a vending machine."

"Time is what keeps everything from happening at once."

"I love cats... they taste just like chicken"

"Out of my mind. Back in five minutes."

"Forget the Joneses. I keep up with the Simpsons."

"Born Free .....Taxed to Death"

"Cover me. I'm changing lanes."

"As long as there are tests, there will be prayer in public schools"

"The more people I meet, the more I like my dog."

"Laugh alone and the world thinks you're an idiot."

"REHAB is for quitters"

"I get enough exercise just pushing my luck!"

"Sometimes I wake up grumpy; Other times I let her sleep"

"All men are Idiots, and I married their King!"

"Jack Kevorkian for White House Physician"

"SAVE A TREE: Eat a beaver"

"Work is for people who don't know how to fish"

"Women who seek to be equal to men lack ambition."

"Your kid may be an honor student, but you're still an IDIOT!"

"It's as BAD as you think, and they ARE out to get you."

"If you don't like the news, go out and make some."

"I Brake For No Apparent Reason."

"When you do a good deed, get a receipt, in case heaven is like the IRS."

"Sorry, I don't date outside my species."

"Nobody's ugly after 2 a.m.!"

"Friends don't let Friends drive Naked."

"Wink, I'll do the rest!"

"No Radio - Already Stolen"

"Reality is a crutch for people who can't handle drugs."

"I took an IQ test, and the results were negative."

"When there's a will, I want to be in it!"

"Okay, who stopped the payment on my reality check?"

"If we aren't supposed to eat animals, why are they made of meat?"

"Few women admit their age. Few men act it!"

"I'm as confused as a baby in a topless bar!"

"I don't suffer from insanity, I enjoy every minute of it!"

"Learn from your parents mistakes - use birth control!"

"Hard work has a future payoff. Laziness pays off NOW!"

"Tell me to 'Stuff It' - I'm a taxidermist."

"IRS: We've got what it takes to take what you have got."

"Time is the best teacher. Unfortunately, it kills all its pupils."

Promote your business through public speaking at every opportunity. Remember, the effectiveness of your speech will depend not only on substantive content but also on your style and manner of delivery.

Chapter 18
Free Ink as Way of Life

"Free ink" is a cryptic phrase. It was doubtless coined by the doubletalk artist who used "insertion" to describe the act of dumping a bunch of armed people from a helicopter several kilometers from where they thought they were supposed to be. What the term refers to is publicity that you don't have to pay for. That part is easy. How to get it where it can be read, viewed or heard by the public is the problem.

Among the pits, pratfalls, and boondoggles routinely encountered by businessmen, none is more a source of neglect and mismanagement than company publicity and public relations programs.

The worst of all possible sins is the one of omission - to do nothing - and, a staggering number of companies do just that. They completely discard the need for a public relations program. It is an escalating folly linked to the times. It is a tough world out there, and it gets meaner and more complicated daily. Washington long ago recognized the need for positive "spin." So must you.

Consumer groups, like fanged cattle, will come for your scalp in galumphing herds if they so much as entertain a suspicion that you may be taking them down the yellow brick road. Anyone who has fallen afoul of OSHA's mandates needs no reminder of the agency's inexhaustible potential for mischief. Should you raise your ceiling or lower your floor? Should you install handrails or trampolines in the employee restroom? How much time is lost by how many businessmen over such trivial considerations as these?

Beyond all this is a new disquiet among Americans - a sullen and often shrill distrust of businesses, profoundly exacerbated by the likes of the Enron, Tyco, and WorldCom debacles.

Ignoring all of this is much like bounding into a snake pit with an aerosol of mace. The following guidelines should help you define and refine your business image – and, more importantly, make it known to your customers, your community, and to the many agencies holding the authority to alternately harass or assist you. Take heed, therefore, to the following:

The Right People/The Right Stuff

Unless your business is very large and intricately diversified, look inside your own shop for PR talent. If you employ a half dozen or more college-educated professionals, chances are excellent that you'll find among them some latent talent for journalism and PR contact. Good news releases are just not that hard to prepare. They require a feeling of what is or is not news, rudiments of talent in good timing, and a common sense approach to priorities. One of your bright-eyed, bushy-tailed lieutenants with a flair for concise memos could be a natural.

You have an advantage if you learn to play a bit on healthy human vanity. Your mid-level administrator, suddenly appointed director of publicity, is likely to give the assignment his or her best effort. Media contact and the occasional opportunity for a byline or internal recognition make for heady stuff - unless your appointee is over eighty, dead, loathes you, or has a better job offer. Just make sure that you review the material prepared or delegate the job to someone you trust as much as your Mama.

You also want to avoid the trap of giving your PR person full rein as company spokesman, unless you fully trust her judgment to speak with authority on vital issues important to your business operation.

When is your company big enough to require a professional PR agency? Only you can answer that. If your operation is large, complex, diversified, or if it faces specific public relations difficulties, you may need a professional PR agency.

Publicity and public relations are largely intangibles, though progressive firms will spend as much or more time in follow-up on your publicity and image as they do preparing and disturbing materials on it. However, be sure to enter an arrangement with a PR firm the same way you conduct any other business. Investigate the firm's reputation. Compare their rates. Ask for other client referrals, and check them. Demand to see concrete results the PR firm has gained for businesses similar to yours. Find out who would be responsible for handing your account, and interview that individual with the same keen eye you'd cast on one of your own executive applicants. Get proposals in writing, keep them on file, review them as necessary, and rattle sabers if performance does not match promises. They'll respect you for it and will work harder for your company.

Once you've worked through to a decision on how to set up your publicity program, your new administrator will want to look for the kinds of things that are news and can be used to benefit your business.

New employees are a natural. They're excited (or at least vaguely optimistic) about coming to work for you. That's news. They'll spend money in your community, join churches, clubs and civic groups, and they'll represent you to the extent that the job you've given them provides that complex and important thing called positive self-image.

If your new person is worth having aboard, they are enthusiastic and interested in their new job and so are their friends and associates and the community at large. The key here is to do things right and do them as they join you - not six expectant and disappointed months down the road.

Get the necessary facts in the release. Sure, his or her professional and educational background is important, but don't stop at that. Maybe the guy has a Navy Cross in his dresser drawer. Maybe she's a Rhodes Scholar. He might have nailed the last hole-in-one at Pinehurst. She may have written a novel and sold it. He may have a vintage Porsche in his garage that he restored by hand. Within reason, look for those human dimensions that make every individual unique and versatile. The proper discovery could convert a routine release on a new worker into genuine feature material, good for the six o'clock news and a photo spread in the Daily Blat. Such media exposure on good people is seldom divorced from their connection with your business. It lights the lamp at tunnel's end.

A continuing search for legitimate opportunity for positive public messages is the real job of your PR officer or firm. Think angles. And, while you are thinking, don't neglect the people who have been with you for years. They achieve, they accomplish, and their lives continue to change in interesting ways. Monitor those changes, connect them to the company name, and the results will be both widely seen and heard.

If your company is surviving in business, you'll routinely gain new contracts and probably will develop new product lines. Publicize them wisely, and they'll pay in media response. A contract for 500 new grandfather clocks is not news or ho-hum news at best. But, what if your PR genius discovers it's the biggest contract yet for that item in your state or marketing zone? That, as they say, is a different story.

If the product or service you offer does not provide some unique or at least competitive attraction to consumers, chances are good you're reading this book out of nostalgia. New product lines are developed to do something bigger, better, longer, faster, or cheaper. That's news. The imagination, clarity, and degree of topical interest applied to the information generated on product features will go a long way toward getting you some free ink.

Your own PR people have to maintain a delicate relationship with those who will ultimately decide if your news will be printed or broadcast. First put your best people forward. They should be creative initiators, sincere about their PR assignments and ruthlessly candid about the way they handle them. Nothing is sadder than the limp remains of a slick-shoe hype artist or glad handed phony after a grizzled city desk editor or TV news director had him for lunch and spat his remains out the rear doorway.

Do not attempt to shove trivia at your media contact. They'll toss it out and come to expect nothing from your people but drivel. Give them substance, something into which they can sink their journalistic teeth.

Never, *repeat,* never attempt to force a commitment from an editor or reporter. They know news. If your people have a well prepared, concisely written release of general interest to the public, your news will compete on its own merit with other news of the day for print space or broadcast time.

Again, seek the angles. Recognize the potential for news within your staff and company. Go after it. Treat public relations and publicity with the same honesty and enthusiasm you conduct other business. Keep your best people out front.

Respect the media. It may just be this country's most powerful and unique motivating force, and your business is singularly unique if it can afford to do without it.

Press Interviews

Always try to anticipate the questions that will be asked, which is easier to do than you may realize. Do not let the interviewer, who is extremely experienced in interviewing techniques, make you look silly by asking a question with a premise already implied, such as, "Does your mother know you smoke weed?"

The best technique is simply a short statement to the effect that the question implies a premise which is untrue. Be sure not to dwell on this, and move quickly to another subject in a smooth manner.

Another thing to watch, and I strongly suggest this, is that the interviewer's question be answered directly, such as "Yes, we have had an accident in the plant during the year," and then go into the circumstances around the accident and the reasons it might not have been avoidable.

This runs against all the techniques you have learned in business in that you typically give all the facts, the alternatives, and then your recommended solutions when approaching a business problem.

As to live television interviews, they're like soccer in a minefield. You may get the first kick in, but the rest of the game can be hairy, especially since it is customary in the TV industry to shoot the wounded. Television interviewers are a distinct breed. You don't run into much of this unless the interviewer is Bill O'Reilly. In that instance it will do little good to either anticipate questions or to carefully formulate your answers to them. This breed generally has the attention span of a burst of hair spray. While you are in the verbal throes of your answer to their last question, they're making up the next one. They have the singular ability to read aloud a news report, giving it the drama and intensity of an eyewitness, while having not the vaguest notion of what it means.

Freezing up on television during an interview is much like discovering that you arrived drunk at a Salvation Army testimonial dinner, and you were scheduled as the keynote speaker. The interviewer will seize such an opportunity as if it were fine gold, bombarding you with three replacement questions more dreadful than the one you've choked on. The silences are terrible.

The prepared statement is a partial defense against televised interviews. If you write your own statement, though, you should be reminded of the old adage concerning fools who are their own lawyers. Nothing is worse than reading a prepared statement, ostensibly your own sincere words, than stuttering through the whole mess.

The terrible red eye of the camera can undo in an instant even the most suave and practiced. I have a broadcasting acquaintance who used to do TV commercials live on breaks during a western theatre. His product on one fateful Saturday afternoon was 'Faultless Starch." He will never forget the instant he smiled, faced the camera and intoned: "... and now, ladies and gentlemen, a word from our sponsor: Fartless Storch."

Trade Journals

An important forum in which the manufacturer and distributor can impress the retailer, and vice versa, is the industry trade journal, whether in electronic or print form.

While the manufacturer and the distributor have the use of advertising (which many retailers claim is read only by the manufacturer's competition), the retailer, like the manufacturer and distributor, can convey the image of desirability of his company in a number of ways.

Perhaps the most impressive is the publication of articles about the industry, or about improvements of business methods. As a writer, you can take the simple and make it complicated and mysterious, as most business writers unfortunately do, or you can, like John Steinbeck, use clear and concise language. As you write your article, remember that basic business principles remain intact over the decades, save for some fraying of the edges, and that these basic principles are applicable in any business or any industry. Hence, you need not search out new concepts in order to write your article. You simply will be telling the businessman what he already knows, but your reminder will rejuvenate and reinforce his mind, and he will find the article both helpful and useful.

Press releases, whether drafted by retailer, manufacturer, or distributor, are also effective in creating a positive company image. Naturally, the release should be written with care. A picture, diagram, map, or some other visual aid should definitely accompany it. The art should also be of superior quality.

Letters to the editor can be a strong image builder for your small business. This is perhaps the best way you can show your expertise and common sense through the medium of the trade journal. Don't dodge controversy in writing to the editor. Controversial subject matter is not harmful if you are on the same side of the issue as the reader! You can also write editorial letters of praise and goodwill, or even plant "seeds" like Johnny did from Ohio to Virginia.

Keep the editorial letter brief and to the point. An opening flowery paragraph about the positive virtues and accomplishments of your company will violate the rule of brevity. Most papers limit letters to 300 words, which doesn't leave much room for a long-winded opening paragraph.

The manufacturer, distributor and retailer have common interest in a trade journal beyond the creation of goodwill. The leading industry trade journal is an excellent source for management people in the job market. This necessitates a good relationship with the editor and publisher. You might even consider inviting the principals and their wives down for a weekend of sailing.

The trade journal is an excellent source of industry history which you may need from time to time. It is an extremely good source of fresh information concerning the people from whom you buy, the people to whom you sell, and your competition. You will have to filter out the propaganda, but the news article will give you information about your competition, buyers, and suppliers that you can use in making sound management decisions. This is the main reason trade journals are required management reading. Also, you, like the cynical retailer suggests, may want to read the ads of your competitors to make sure you know what they are up to.

Blogs have added a new, powerful dimension to extend business communication. I offer my blog as an example: Web2ohTV.com.

Finally, if your small business goes belly-up, you may need the help of the editor of the trade journal in getting a new job before your unemployment benefits lapse...

Chapter 19
Oh Wad Some Pow'r the Giftie Gie Us,
To See Ourselves As Others See Us
~Robert Burns~

Good trial lawyers spend a great deal of time on both their own appearance – literally, how they look - before the jury and with their client's appearance. Special emphasis should be placed on clothing. These courtroom attorneys fully appreciate the impact a person's dress and appearance have on others, particularly if that person is a defendant in a heinous crime. The importance of dress is not fully appreciated in the business community, and if clothes don't make the person, they certainly make the businessperson. This isn't as much a lack of appreciation of the importance of clothes as it is the fact that those in business frequently let their spouse select their wardrobe. This is not good. The wardrobe may please the spouse, but it frequently isn't the proper dress for the corporate establishment.

To be a positive authoritative symbol, there are two basic rules for dressing: (1) dress conservatively and traditionally, and, (2) make sure the clothes are tailored to fit you precisely. Conservative and traditional is not a loud, checked sport coat with a white belt and matching white shoes with buckles, topped off with a hand-painted mermaid tie that isn't properly tied. Tailored-to-fit does not mean double breaks in the creases of the skirt, wadded waistbands, and coat breaks at the top of the arm.

As surely as scrambled eggs on the cap visor denotes rank in the military, conservative and traditional dress connotes authority and power in the business world. If what you wear is seemingly unimportant, consider this: I know a purchasing agent who admits closing his mind to a marketing director's proposal on a $2 million office machinery deal because the sales executive wore white socks and an identification bracelet. Clark, the hapless businessman in the National Lampoon vacation movies, should not be your idol.

A trip to the haberdasher who caters to the carriage trade is in order for the small businessman. Such a haberdasher, of course, will have a tailor. Men, you should purchase shoes in the $400 range, dark brown or black, fine grain and wing-tipped. You only need a dozen pairs of long, stretch, quality dress stocks. The stretch will allow the socks to stand up during normal management activities. The entire dozen pairs should be black, which will eliminate the pairing problem. Jettison the florescent ties painted with hula skirts, and purchase three ties with or without embossed design in a solid color - solid blue, solid maroon, and solid dark brown. Stay away from prints. Good silk is recommended because budget ties look like budget ties. One diagonally striped "Rep" tie, and one with small, understated polka dots are also suitable.

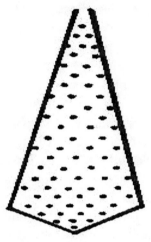

For women and men, the best shirt is still the white shirt, although pale blue is also acceptable. The reasoning behind this is sound: the shirt is merely a background for a tie. If you prefer, pin-striped shirts serve a purpose, but use no more than two colors, and keep the stripe extra thin.

A monogram on a white shirt imparts authority. Monograms on shirt sleeves, particularly in loud colors, however, are as gauche as the 1950's fad of rolling a cigarette pack in the arm of a tee shirt. Pendants, Indian rings and bracelets, rings with precious stones, diamond stickpins and similar flashy adornments are suspect in business circles.

For both sexes, the suit is the most important item. It creates an image of authority. Keep in mind that the power colors are dark charcoal grey and dark blue. Black is not advisable unless you are either a pallbearer or the pall (a waste, I might add, of a perfectly good suit...). Again, make absolutely sure the suit is tailored to fit you perfectly.

I don't want to leave the impression that one shouldn't own sport coats. To the contrary, sport coats are quite acceptable at casual social outings. A Joseph coat of many colors, however, is suggested only when you are comatose and want to alert other guests as you approach. You might consider carrying a portable disco ball to complete the spectacle.

A *Wall Street Journal* interview with Herbert T. Mines, president of the recruiting firm "Business Careers", cites a good example of the importance of proper tailoring. After listing poor dress or grooming as major reasons why candidates fail to land high-level management jobs, he notes that being well-dressed includes more than wearing fashionable or expensive clothes. One candidate was rejected, he says, simply because his costly, vested suit made him appear overweight. Appearances, it seems, are still everything.

Again, for both women and men, avoid the common tendency to purchase suits that look alike. Your business associates may suppose you're wearing the same suit every day. They may begin to question your hygiene. Instead, purchase one solid suit in each of the basic power colors, with one of the three suits vested. To expand your conservative and traditional wardrobe, it is appropriate to select one suit with a hairline vertical pin stripe (the choice of aristocrats) and one patterned suit in a plaid rather than checks, with the pattern extremely subdued and in the general colors of the basic suits.

If you need vision correction, wide latitude is permitted in selecting the style of your eyeglasses. Clear plastic frames or slightly rounded horn-rims are the most accepted. The image of Bob Cratchet in his square wire glasses and green visor might make you want to avoid wire frames. Tinted lenses are gauche.

Conservative corporate dress tells those you meet that you are in your war armor. High style tailoring tells observers that, judging by your dress, a social event is probably in the offing - certainly not hard work. The business world would be ill-at-ease with Beau Brummell. The conservative cut of corporate dress enhances the stoical, no-nonsense approach you are striving for as a small businessman. It comforts the attitudes of the corporate establishment. These principles apply equally to the many women executives now entering management.

If you are in a business that does not require formal business attire, the foregoing principles nevertheless apply to those occasions which call for it. Otherwise, keep your business style clean, neat and low key, regardless of what business you are in.

Image equals credibility – always. Wear your clothes well. Don't let your clothes wear you!

The Physique (Yes, the Outside Counts!)

More important even than dress, the physical shape of the business man or woman must be lean. This, more than anything else, tells others that you are stoical. It proves that you have discipline, that you are active, and that you are ready for combat.

Since weight is something which most individuals can control, excessive poundage is poor advertisement. Height is helpful, but unfortunately this factor is in the hands of another. Height is a positive authoritative symbol. The best advice for those who are on the dwarfish side is to do like Napoleon and stay on your horse at all times.

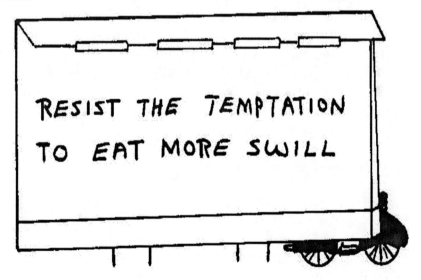

Roadsign urging all to shed pounds

The way to stay in fighting shape is simply to take in no more calories than the body expends. Cut down on the swill.

The *Wizard of Id* by permission of Johnny Hart and Field Enterprises, Inc.

Easily said, huh? Both diet and physical activity are, quite possibly, overrated. The problem with dieting is that it keeps your mind on weight, and the problem with physical exercise is that it expands some people's appetite.

A particular problem is faced by the manager who spends most of his or her day behind a desk. Too many of these people fail to realize, despite conventional wisdom, that calories can, indeed, be burned off in the hundreds by engaging in strenuous exercises that are common for office workers. The following is a list of calorie-burning activities you can effectively put into practice without leaving the comfort of your office chair, followed by the number of calories per activity you can burn:

Jumping on someone's backside 75
Jogging your memory 125
Jumping to conclusions 100
Climbing the walls 150
Swallowing your pride 50
Passing the buck 25
Grasping at straws 75
Beating your own drum 100
Throwing your weight around 50-300 (depends on your heft...)
Dragging your heels 100

Pushing your luck 250
Making mountains out of molehills 500
Spinning your wheels 175
Flying off the handle 225
Hitting the nail on the head 50
Turning the other cheek 75
Wading through paperwork 300
Bending over backwards 75
Rolling heads 200
Balancing the books 23
Beating your head against a wall 150
Running around in circles 350
Chewing nails 200
Eating crow 200
Fishing for compliments 225
Tooting your own horn 25
Climbing the ladder of success at Goolsby's place 750
Pulling out the stops 75
Adding fuel to the fire 150
Pouring salt on the wound 50
Wrapping it up at day's end 12

You might consider buying a full-length mirror for your bathroom, which will keep your amorphous shape in view. Gazing constantly at the reflection of a human squash plant will give you the necessary willpower to lose weight. Also, consider cutting out breakfast, which will contract your stomach during the day. In a typical day, coffee with sugar and cream omitted will eliminate calories. The taste won't be missed since the daily pressures anesthetize your taste buds anyway. Some authorities suggest taking turns with your wife in carrying each other around the house, or spend 15 minutes each morning jogging with a goat. Heck, do like a buddy of mine who hops to work on one foot and hops home on the other.

It is best to use a program of basic calisthenics even if you play the more strenuous sports like tennis, touch football, canoeing and basketball. Even in such sports as these, a great deal of time is spent doing nothing. Much more time in tennis, considered to be one of the more strenuous sports, is spent retrieving tennis balls and preparing to receive serves, than is spent in actually moving to or hitting the ball. Too, tennis may involve driving miles to a court, paying high fees, searching for a partner and arranging schedules, all of which may put a damper on regular participation.

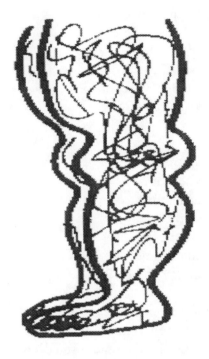

Your legs after jogging

Jogging is excellent exercise. Its activity is constant; it exerts many muscles and enhances cardiovascular fitness as well as keeping you trim. Consider this specimen:

Jumping rope is the best exercise, having all the advantages of jogging without being susceptible to inclement weather or jogger's nipples.

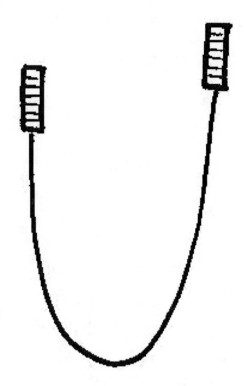

Either of the foregoing two exercises will enable the businessperson to get a vigorous workout in a short period of time, control weight, and not lull her into thinking she can overeat with the justification that she has just done an abundance of exercise, as might have been the case had she played two sets of tennis. In fact, she would have done more waiting than exercising! Too, you must consider the amount of time you will save by substituting these exercise activities for other sports, time that can be applied to business endeavors.

In the alternative, one might also consider sex. It's convenient, inexpensive, and fun. In this age of products which overcome erectile dysfunction, there is no excuse. There are numerous medications for headaches and legal stimulants which obviate the "I'm too tired" line of avoidance.

Extended foreplay followed by strenuous lovemaking followed by extended foreplay followed by......well, you get the idea....is ideal. Calories will be burned.

This activity is not recommended for the office, however.

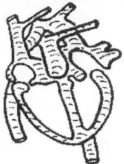

**20 HP Executive Heart: 110 RPMs Recommended
Maximum**
(except during intercourse…)

Although I know of no studies concerning the weight of top executives in either large or small businesses, I consider it to be common knowledge that there exists an extremely high correlation between trimness and those men and women in top management.

Executive Stress
In addition to keeping you trim, exercise and a proper diet will reduce your chances of coronary artery disease and heart attacks, the major cause of death among Americans. Moreover, exercise relieves stress!

By far the major factor in increasing the risk of coronary artery disease is the presence of the "Type A" personality - the highly competitive and hard-driving person. The more responsibility you carry for the performance of people, the greater your stress and the higher your risk of heart disorder.

If you have a family history of heart attacks, hypertension, elevated blood cholesterol, or if you smoke cigarettes, the extremely high stress of owning and managing a business is enough to put you at extreme risk.

Annual Physical For Executives
Even though there is a current headlong rush by company executives to undergo annual physical examinations as preventive health maintenance, physicals are not always the most effective means of maintaining health and monitoring potential heart disease.

Research indicates that periodic health exams do not necessarily produce fewer deaths, less disease or less disability. Some believe that the call for periodic health exams is initiated by physicians and not necessarily the result of specific health issues, complaints or concerns. In short, a physical exam may give a patient a relatively meaningless feeling of reassurance that all life systems are go for one year or 12,000 miles, but death as a result of failing health voids the warranty . Instead, combine maintenance of your body, soul and spirit with periodic physicals. Be pro-active in keeping your health. You do it for your car, don't you? The better you maintain your vehicle, the fewer visits to the mechanic...

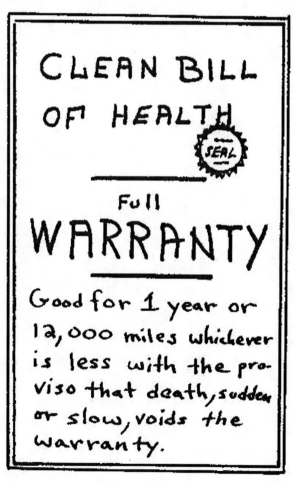

As a small business owner/manager, you will find that the stress you try to avoid, but frequently cannot, will wind you up like a clock, and cause some sleepless nights. There are things you can do to help yourself. You will find that going to bed and waking up at the same time each day, including Saturday and Sunday, will minimize insomnia. Waking at the same time is more important than what time you go to bed. This will be more helpful in getting good nights of sleep than counting sheep or popping pills. Sleep is a balm to your health. Finally, you can avoid flu and colds if you keep your hands washed. Germs are passed in the business world through handshakes.

Thank you, Doctor Johnston...

Chapter 20
Going with the Over the Hill Gang

It is fashionable for business executives to cater to and promote youthful management. However, this practice - though fashionable - is plainly in error. Youth is especially undesirable in your selection of outside consultants, particularly attorneys, for youth frequently fails to see the subtlety of a transaction. Instead, look for outside professional people with the most hash marks.

In a World Series game, a young manager attempted what he thought to be a wise tactic. When one of his veteran hitters reached first base in a close game, the manager substituted a pinch runner who was one of the fastest men ever to run in national track and field events. But, the substitute had not learned the subtle and crafty art of base-running. He was picked off at first base by the pitcher. The young manager had outsmarted himself.

The judgment and experience of an older consultant, businessman or attorney is preferred over youth, all other things being equal - which they rarely are. Nothing gives a small business owner greater security than the presence of a bald counselor whose temples are gray and whose eyes are crinkled with crow's feet, whose only social chit-chat is an exclamation that, "Mother loved me but she died."

Octogenarian D.C. super-lawyer Clark Clifford epitomizes the experience and judgment of an older counselor. Advisor and confidant to four presidents, his expertise gained through years of experience is well known, and, it should be added, expensive. Rightfully so. The older the antique, the more valuable it becomes.

The story goes that the president of a large corporation sought Clifford's advice about a problem with a government agency. After analyzing the problem, Clifford advised the executive to do absolutely nothing and sent a bill for $16,000. The bill and the advice shocked the executive. Why, he quizzed, should he do nothing? "Because I told you so," Clifford supposedly said and tacked on an additional two grand to his bill.

As a small businessman you might want to use the following sources to gather free information before using your outside professional people:

Some newspapers have toll-free lines which will answer questions. "What Federal Agency inspects dams?" "Can I use an undisclosed tape recorded conversation as evidence against a supplier?" "Can my employees' wages be garnished?"

Also, most government agencies have toll-free lines. For example, you can receive tax advice which you should also treat as preliminary from the regional Internal Revenue Service. "If we open a cafeteria and subsidize part of the food cost, will this be reportable income to our employees?"

Maintain your anonymity lest you trigger an audit on yourself by the question. There is no doubt in my mind that some of the information you confide to a government official during an interview gets back to your dossier. Just behind "the check is in the mail" are the second and third biggest lies: "I'm from the government and I'm here to help you" and "I'm progressive; I can handle change."

There are a number of columnists who answer questions. "Our company plans to buy some preferred stock, the dividends of which are 85% tax free to the corporation. What three issues with dividend rates over 6% in the New York State do you recommend?" "We plan to borrow some 90-day money in six months. Should we lock in our cost by buying a Treasury bill future?"

Lastly, most libraries are extremely cooperative. "Could you send me any recent pamphlets on industrial revenue bonds?" "What is your best book on the registration and protection of trademarks?" Next go on the internet. Then consult with your outside professional people.

In selecting a certified public accountant, experience and expertise is essential. Just as you cannot fly blind, you cannot run a business without properly maintained financial record books from which your accountant can draw frequent financial statements showing what you have done and where you are.

Financial statements consist of a balance sheet listing the company's resources together with the interests of the creditors and owners in those resources, and a profit and loss statement to tell you how much you sold, how much you spent in the process, and where you spent it, and whether or not you have anything left over to live *la dolce vita.*

During your consideration of a certified public accountant, who will be an extremely important outsider to your company, ask him the answer to the problem of "two plus two." If he replies, "Have you any particular number in mind?" be duly impressed and continue to test him with these doodles before making your final selection:

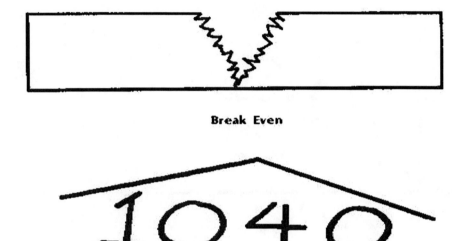

Break Even

Tax Shelter

Proper accounting is essential to the successful operation of an independent business. Take care of it well from the beginning. Important as it is, the cost of accounting is one of the smallest expenses of doing business. Get the best you can buy, and don't worry about what it costs.

Don't select for an investment counselor a golfing buddy whose only area of competency is government bonds. Avoid economists who churn out sweeping economic forecasts fit only for the wastebasket. Find an outside economist who can ply his skills to your company and industry. Even then, keep in mind Arthur H. Motley's comment that if the nation's economists were laid end to end, they would still point in all directions. Remember, too, in 1929 the late Irving Fisher of Yale, then among the most eminent economists in the U.S., said that business prospects appeared good. As your small business grows, you and your company will need the best guidance possible on stocks, municipal bonds, mergers, economics, and commodities. To test their experience and competency, ask the economist and investment counselor to interpret the graph below.

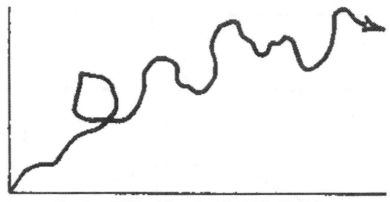

Random Walk of Drunken Portfolio Manager

In selecting an attorney, do not make the common mistake of picking Mr. Womble just because Smith, Jamison, Cohn, Womble, Lucas (and the third army) is a big firm, or, the firm of Lawless & Lynch has always handled your family's legal affairs. If you have a choice between the better facts or the better attorney than your opponent in a legal proceeding, the more clever attorney should be your pick.

The system of unequal justice under lawyers suffers from a wide disparity of legal talent. Some lawyers are superior while others are *per se* violations of the Sixth Amendment, which guarantees the right to (effective) counsel. With an unbelievable one out of every 500 people being an attorney: 462,000 U.S. lawyers - you have at least the benefit of a large selection. Do your homework. Select the best lawyer.

Use these doodles to aid you in selecting counsel who knows the red-eye law:

Escrow

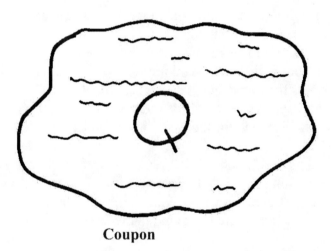

Coupon

Chapter 21
Dipping into the Classics

I believe in the Renaissance man rather than in the technocrat. It is my feeling that one's primary source of management inspiration will come from reading the classics. *Tess of the D'urbervilles* and *David Copperfield* will give you as much insight into understanding the people and events of business as anything Peter Drucker put into a textbook. *"Attach and Die"* by Grady McWhiney and Perry D. Jamieson is truly the *best business book* ever written.

Moreover, what we call management classics, such as *Galbraith's Great Crash of* 1929, and Whyte's *The Organization Man,* can be equally enlightening. Let us read at least two classics a year. Even though there remain many good contemporary best sellers, only time can rank them as classics.

I found that law school prepared me substantially better for business than graduate business school. The study of law forces you to dig deeply in the well of information and fully discern the facts. Fully understanding the facts helps turn a complex decision into a reflex.

That said, I submit that reading the following books is the best preparation for the challenges of business, especially in dealing with strategy at a corporate governance level. These Hall of Fame books for the most part are not found in the business section of the library.

BOOKS ON BUSINESS STRATEGY

Non-Business Books

Attach and Die by Grady McWhiney and Perry D. Jamieson (1982)

This obscure book teaches the importance of understanding how new technology and an understanding of the ever-changing situation and facts impact strategic decision making and how prior success may reinforce a bias even though the situation and technology have changed. If you are only going to read one of those books, this masterpiece on strategic thinking should be your choice.

The Guns of August by Barbara Tuchman (1962)

Élan is not a strategy. Being more intelligent and working harder than your competition is an unacceptable strategy. This Book also teaches the importance of contingency planning.

Zen and the Art of Motorcycle Maintenance by Robert Pirsig (1974)

You best understand the mind of the Woodstock generation when selling goods and offering services to that generation. They are older now, but their attitude, outlook and beliefs tend to remain.

The Autobiography of Malcolm X by Malcolm X (1964)

This incredible book sears into your brain that others see the world differently from you. Your peers may view the world much as you do, but we all need to be reminded that many others see and experience the world quite differently.

Class by Paul Fussell (1983)

This book debunks the myth that there can be a classless society. America has a class system that at times can make India look egalitarian. You don't need to read this page-turner if you know what is the major determination of class in America.

All Quiet on the Western Front by Erich Remarque (1929)

Compare this book to "The Red Badge of Courage" written by a minister's son who never held a rifle, much less fired one. This masterpiece shows why there is no substitute for first hand experience learned in the trenches of life. It changed my life.

Mind of the South by W. J. Cash (1941)

Let's just say you cannot really maximize your sales below the Mason Dixon line without the benefit of this watershed sociology book. It is also a reminder that one can sometimes arrive at correct conclusions through the art of observation and without the benefit of empirical research.

Tess of the d'Urbervilles by Thomas Hardy (1891)

To be effective, in dealing with people it is important to know their origins. And, yes, status is not politically correct but is nevertheless weaved into business.

Class of 1846 by John Waugh (1994)

Average intelligence and sheer grit personified in General Stonewall Jackson pummeled superior intellect lacking tenacity, personified by General George McClellan.

Scott's Last Expedition by Robert Falcon Scott (1914) and *The South Pole* by Captain Roald Amundsen (1912)

There is no better leadership case study, ever, than placing the diaries of these two explorers side by side. The contrast of success (Amundson) and failure (Scott) in these classics could not be starker. For additional case studies in leadership, I also recommend the journeys of the following two explorers: *The Worst Journey in the World* by Apsley Cherry-Garrard (1922) and *The Last Place on Earth* by R. Huntford (1986)

Nine Nations of North America by Joel Garreau (1981)

Our country is not one nation, but many when it comes to business dealings.

The Picture of Dorian Grey by Oscar Wilde (1890)

The absence of regimentation and discipline leads to a non-productive life no matter how clever you might be.

Moby Dick by Herman Melville (1851)

Obsession with revenge is destructive. Move on.

The Iliad by Homer (in the 700's BC)

Teamwork is important but so is leadership. (Painfully read in Greek for a grade and in English for the many strategic building blocks).

The Longest Day by Cornelius Ryan (1959)

The element of surprise is underrated - especially in strategy.

The Tipping Point: How Little Things Can Make a Big Difference by Malcolm Gladwell (2000)

This book explores how details can make a big difference. How ideas and group behaviors can tip a product, service or fad into a national best seller or phenomena.

Lincoln on Leadership by Donald T. Phillips (1992)

Deep insight into events and people are essential for successful strategy.

In the Heart of the Sea by Nathaniel Philbrick (2000)

The odyssey of the Nantucket whaling ship, Essex, is a study in how multiple bad decisions cascade into catastrophe. Fortune Magazine recognized this book as one of the great *business* books. Pathology is a great teacher!

1984 by George Orwell (1949)

This frightening portrait of a society that destroys privacy and distorts truth is a reminder that values and beliefs must be a part of any corporate strategy.

Alexander Hamilton by Ron Chernon

Values and principles are indeed important for individualism business and government. Equal to Presidents Adams, Jefferson, Madison and Monroe in his understanding of concepts of governments, Hamilton surpassed these presidents with his profound understanding of commerce, banking, industry and entrepreneurship.

Business Books

There are select groups of business books that directors and management with genuine interest in strategy may want to read:

Crossing the Chasm by Geoffrey Moore (1991)

This classic teaches how to target a new technology or service to early adopters and figure out how to mass market it. By the way, diagrams as used herein are most helpful in big picture thinking for your company.

Positioning, the Battle for Your Mind by Reis and Trout (1981)

If you understand why no one knows the name of the second man to fly the Atlantic solo, then you can skip this best seller.

The Wealth of Nations by Adam Smith (1776)

I hope our grandchildren's grandchildren will also read this eloquent proposition of liberty, enlightened government, and worth of the individual in support of the morality of capitalism. In my 41 years in the business world at the board level, the number one failing of corporate America I have seen is that employees are not coached as to how his or her job really benefits customers and humankind.

Fire in the Belly by Jerry D. Neal (2005)

With high drama, the author shows the challenges and trauma of taking a concept to start-up and ultimately to a billion dollar public company. You will feel the agony and ecstasy as though you, too, wore crampons along with the other RF Micro Devices founders.

Leading the Revolution by Gary Hamel (2000)

This volume teaches how to think strategically about everything. It includes many excellent case studies. When finished, you will begin to think strategically about boiling an egg.

My Years at General Motors by Alfred P. Sloan (1963)

This is my favorite business book, really the history of industrial America as well as the organization of management and business entities for effectiveness.

However, if you are that one who finds the classics unbearable, possibly as a result of the way these great books were approached like a Latin course, understand that most best sellers are better than no reading at all, excepting, perhaps, potboilers of the Harold Robbins variety. If, however, you simply can't tolerate reading anything that doesn't come in glossy format, read on. There's still hope for you.

Chapter 22
Dipping into the Newsstands

In the business world, an executive must stay informed not only about what's going on in business but also about the happenings in the contemporary world. In addition to reading your daily newspaper, pick out and concentrate on one magazine of general interest. *Newsweek,* perhaps, or *Time.* You should consider such business publications as the *Wall Street Journal, Fortune, Business Week,* and *Dun's Review,* but choose and read only one. Avoid the *Kiplinger Washington Letter,* whose economic predictions, for the most part, are superficial. You can trap yourself into too much current events reading and sacrifice your productivity as a manager/owner. It would also impose on your own personal time.

It is important to understand what you read. Watch the news on television once a day. This can give you a different perspective on what you find in your newspaper. The spoken word often clarifies the written word, enhancing the learning process - the very reason professors lecture about materials in textbooks that a college student is quite obviously free to read for himself. Until his recent death Louis Rukeyser's *Wall Street Week* was compulsory viewing. *Main Street USA* would have better described the broadcast. The business week was concisely reviewed, benefiting large and small business owners alike. Look for similar broadcasts, though Rukeyser's was one of the best and will be sorely missed. Instead, consider *Marketplace,* a nightly business program hosted by Cheryl Glaser on National Public Radio (NPR) stations around the country. This is an excellent program.

Your industry trade journals or the leading journal for your particular industry is "must" reading.

Economics has become an important subject to all business people. It gives insight into the future conditions of the market. Of course, a small business cannot afford to hire a staff economist. Therefore, with economics being such a complicated and vital subject, you should consider subscribing to a monthly economic cassette tape service which a number of ranking financial institutions offer. The complicated subject of economics is put in non-technical language. The business outlook for the near and distant term is clearly explained.

A vast array of economic statistics published mainly by the government and partly by private groups, like the automobile manufacturers, and carried on the commodity futures pages, signal forthcoming trends of various components of the economy. Another example is single-family housing starts statistics, which signal future trends to homebuilders, appliance and furniture manufacturers and retailers, and similar businesses related to the new home market.

Other statistical fine points hidden in the small print can be revealing and give you a sense of assurance as you plan for your small business. One example affecting all small business owners is the outlook for the prime rate - the rate of interest commercial banks charge on short-term loans to their best credit-worthy customers. There is a correlation between the prime rate and the rate on treasury bills. Other rates are scaled upward (skyward, according to many small business owners) from the prime rate. How many times have you seen a banker swivel and rock back in a chair rolling his eyeballs to the ceiling and giving an authoritative-sounding if fallacious answer to the question, "What do you expect the prime rate to do?" Not only is he not an economist, but frequently he proves what Pope knew: *A little learning is a dangerous thing; Drink deep, or taste not the Pierian spring.*

Additionally, rest assured that the banker has not backed his opinion with one cent of his own money.

Henceforth, go to the commodity market quotes in the financial section of the paper, and find the U.S. Treasury bill futures traded on the Chicago Board of Exchange. These Treasury bill futures give insight into interest rate expectations of corporate treasurers and bankers who hedge their borrowing costs, as well as financiers who speculate on the future course of interest rates. In buying these contracts, they are ponying up big money concerning future rates.

The prime rate, historically, has been priced at a premium above the Treasury bill yield. This premium is called a "spread" or "yield differential". This "spread" is determined by market forces, the explanation of which is beyond the scope of this book. You just need to know that these forces exist and have an impact upon your cost of borrowing.

The spread is calculated in "basis points." A basis point is one-one-hundredth of 1 % (0.01 %). Hence, 1 % equals 100 basis points. If Treasury bills are being priced to yield a certain percent at maturity, or, if the *futures* market is predicting they will be sold to yield a certain percent at some set point *in the future,* this is a good indication that your borrowing rate, usually prime plus one or two percent, will be at a level somewhat higher than what the market is predicting Treasury yields will be. Therefore, to get an idea of where the prime rate (and your potential cost of borrowing) is headed, watch the Treasury bill futures.

Perhaps the most revealing form of business statistics, however, is the graph. An imaginative controller can take the most complicated business occurrences and clarify them using a simple graph such as the one on the following page:

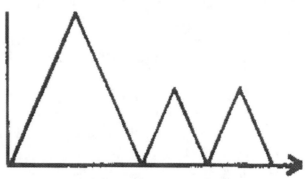

Parent company acquires two smaller companies' manufacturing pyramids.

I fondly refer to the above as "Duh Graph".

Chapter 23
Harassment of the Little Guy by Government

One of the biggest obstacles to success in a small business is the &* ?#!*~#*! ! (expletive deleted) government. The economies of scale favor the large and discriminate against the small business. The time it takes to complete all the government surveys is about the same for a billion dollar business as it is for a million dollar business. This means the cost as a percentage of sales dollars is one thousand times more for the small business. OSHA, EPA, EEOC, DOT and all the rest of the alphabet-soup agencies cost small businesses disproportionately more in compliance measures than they cost large firms. *U S. News & World Report* puts the cost of government regulation and paperwork for just small businesses in the billions of dollars.

In an interview with the *Washington Post,* Billy Carter, small businessman and brother to former President Jimmy Carter, once commented on the harassment and burden of government with a level-headedness absent in our latter day pundits. Here, for your enjoyment are several of his observations:

Billy on welfare: "In Sumter County we have as many people administering welfare and related programs as there are in the rest of the county government. They raise hell if people getting welfare go to work. The trouble with the welfare program is that the more people they have on the payroll the more they hire, and the more they hire the more the director gets."

Billy on unemployment abuse: "When unemployment was at the highest, I needed a man to run a peanut-drying machine. It should have paid $250 to $300 a week. I couldn't hire a single person. They would rather draw $90 in tax-free unemployment benefits every week and pick up food stamps at the same time."

More Billy, this time on federal regulations: "The major complaint I have is that 90 % of the folks they send here to inspect us don't know anything. All of the employees working around the gin had to wear earplugs. So, I had to do the ginning. You see, as the owner, there was no way I could be made to wear earplugs. There are about 80 electric motors on a cotton gin, and the only way you can tell when there is a problem is to hear it. You can't convince OSHA about things like that."

Billy on filling out forms: "Some of these quarterly, semi-annual, and annual reports are a three and four-day job. Some are almost impossible to fill out. When they do an agricultural census, you can almost say the hell with everything else for almost a month because it's going to tie you up that long."

The story goes that a friend of Billy's pondered over a federal government questionnaire about his small business that asked "How many employees do you have, broken down by sex?" After proper reflection, he finally answered, "Not one that I know of. Our main problem here in Plains is alcohol."

In the Declaration of Independence, distinguished representatives of the colonies listed, among others, these grievances against King George III:

"He has erected a multitude of new offices and sent hither swarms of officers to harass our people, and eat out their substance." After two hundred years, the basic grievance by small businesspersons against our government, which is supposed to be the servant of its citizenry, is still ". . . swarms of officers to harass our people, and eat out their substance".

William P. Drake, former chairman and president of the Pennwalt Corp., protested it much more subtly than Billy Carter did. At the conclusion of a Pennwalt annual meeting, Mr. Drake read his own adaptation of a modem version of a famous fable. It is worth the re-telling here:

The Little Red Hen

"Once upon a time, there was a little red hen who scratched about the barnyard until she uncovered some grains of wheat. She called her neighbors and said, "If we plant this wheat, we shall have bread to eat. Who will help me plant it?"

"Not I," said the cow.

"Not I," said the duck.

"Not I," said the pig.

"Not I," said the goose

"Then I will," said the little red hen. And she did. The wheat grew tall and ripened into golden grain. "Who will help me reap my wheat?" asked the little red hen.

"Not I," said the duck.

"Out of my classification," said the pig.

"I'd lose my seniority," said the cow.

"I'd lose my unemployment compensation," said the goose.

"Then I will," said the little red hen, and she did.

At last, it came time to bake the bread. "Who will help me bake the bread?" asked the little red hen.

"That would be overtime for me," said the cow.

"I'd lose my welfare benefits," said the duck.

"I'm a dropout and never learned how," said the pig.

"If I'm to be the only helper, that's discrimination," said the goose.

"Then I will," said the little red hen. And, she did. She baked five loaves and held them up for her neighbors to see. They all wanted some and, in fact, demanded a share. But, the little red hen said, "No, I can eat the five loaves myself."

"Excess profits!" cried the cow.

"Capitalist leech!' screamed the duck.

"I demand equal rights!" yelled the goose.

And, the pig just grunted. And, they painted "unfair" picket signs and marched 'round and 'round the little red hen shouting obscenities.

When the government agent came, he said to the little red hen, "You must not be greedy".

"But I earned the bread!" said the little red hen.

"Exactly," said the agent. "That is the wonderful free enterprise system. Anyone in the barnyard can earn as much as he wants. But, under our modem government regulations, the productive workers must divide their product with the idle."

And they lived happily ever after, including the little red hen who smiled and clucked, "I am grateful! I am grateful!"

But her neighbors wondered why she never again baked any more bread."

The End.

Our economic system has turned from laissez-faire to modified capitalism to what one could term regulated capitalism. Perhaps if the next law put on the books was that all must read Mr. Drake's nursery rhyme, then we might avoid the over-regulation of our economic system before it self-destructs, if not for the sake of your small business, then for the sake of the concept of free enterprise. As *Time* Magazine reported in 1978, "The examples of nations and empires - from ancient Rome to modem Britain - that have been weakened or crushed by the weight of bureaucracy are too numerous to be ignored.

Ultimately, who is to blame for our nation's plight? The President? Congress? Whom do we blame for harassment and over regulation? Since government still remains in the hands of the people, the fault must truly lie with each and every one of us. In the words of the comic strip Pogo: "We have met the enemy, and they is us". Surely, if we, the majority, did not want the bureaucracy and harassment under which we all labor, we would insist on government cooperation with business as is done in Japan. We would start regulating the regulators. We are on the same sled ride to the ocean as was Great Britain in recent years, but it is not too late to reverse our direction. Such is the challenge that faces all of us.

A good place to begin improving government is by instituting a letter or email writing policy to your elected representatives about the costly and heavy regulatory burden and any heavy-handed treatment by government agencies of your small business. Consider this telling case in point: OSHA (a four-letter acronym in any small businessperson's book) demanded that In-Line Inc., a North Carolina construction firm, provide a portable toilet for its crew while they were digging a tunnel under a highway. In the widely reported case, the company argued in vain against OSHA's ridiculous and money squandering demand, saying that the men never complained about using the bathroom at a filling station 50 yards away!

Each person in top management should participate in such a campaign, if they agree. The name, address and phone number of the elected officials representing you and your company should be kept current in the company address book. Even middle-management persons such as foremen or floor managers should

172

become familiar with pending legislation, and then give pens, plain paper, stamps and envelopes or access to e-mail to workers so they can write the elected officials in their city, county, district or state expressing their views freely and without censorship.

Above all, don't sit around and mope, as the small businessperson typically does when harassed. Let your elected representatives know how you feel. Take an example from the following gentleman, who received a letter from the Pennsylvania Department of Environmental Quality regarding wooden structures (referred to as "debris" in the State's letter) which he had allegedly constructed without a permit on a stream on his property, causing downstream flooding after a heavy rain. He received a Cease and Desist order threatening "elevated enforcement action" if he did not immediately remove the "debris" from the stream. Here, in part, is his written response to the errant, albeit well-intentioned State government employee who issued the warning:

"A couple of beavers are in the (State unauthorized) process of constructing and maintaining two wood "debris" dams across...the stream...While I did not pay for, authorize, nor supervise their dam project, I think they would be highly offended that you call their skillful use of nature's building materials "debris"...I can safely say that there is no way you could ever match their dam skills, their dam resourcefulness, their dam ingenuity, their dam persistence, their dam determination and/or their dam work ethic...As to your request, I do not think the beavers are aware they must fill out a dam permit prior to the start of this type of activity...Do you require all beavers throughout the state to conform to said dam request? ...as far as the beavers and I are concerned, this dam case can be referred for more elevated enforcement action right now...why wait? If you want the stream "restored" to a dam free-flow condition, please contact the beavers...Being unable to comply with your dam request, and being unable to contact you on your dam answering machine, I am sending this response to your dam office..."

Your tax dollars at work...

Chapter 24
Steady as She Drifts

It is a source of amazement that the small businessperson is unable to quote such things as his most recent sales and profit, the square footage of his store, and the number of his employees. Even more surprising is that he takes no time to periodically review and study his financial statements.

This is less true at the board level. There are, however, some board members who are financially illiterate. This is inexcusable! When you consider that financial statements are a lagging indicator, it would seem that this is a harsh judgment to levy. But, knowing the five-figure costs of an annual statement for most small businesses and knowing that in business, as in other endeavors of life, the past gives insight into the future, it seems rather ridiculous that each succeeding financial report is simply filed away for the archaeologists to excavate at some far future time. If you are dedicated to transparent management and to communicating information - and one hopes you are - the financials need to be made available to your management cadre *now*. Good or bad, the numbers need to be known if your management is to make quality decisions. Even if your cadre cannot decipher the financials, the symbolism of openness is desirable.

You will want to give your financials to your commercial bank officer whose credit analysis people can then study and sit down with you and thrash through their findings. This exercise will be especially worthwhile if you not only cannot read financials but also are unable to distinguish red from black ink. (Regardless of general belief, our government can discriminate the two colors, but is decidedly fonder of red).

To avoid the possibility of a clerk or bank official divulging any of the information in your financial statements, you can protect your privacy by boldly writing in red across the face of the statement:

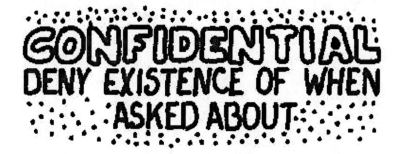

CONFIDENTIAL
DENY EXISTENCE OF WHEN
ASKED ABOUT

With few exceptions, small businesses have almost insatiable money needs. How, then, might you give adequate credit information to your potential vendors and still not make them privy to your confidential financials? Credit people typically give potential debtors the benefit of the doubt when numbers are not available. Once you give out your statements, and later, for any reason, decide your figures are nobody's business, the failure to further submit your statements is considered very negative credit information.

You will not want to give any financial statements to your vendors from the outset, or to Dun & Bradstreet, or Lyons, unless you want a degree from IRS U. That, of course, is the Internal Revenue Service University, where learning is by hard knocks even though the tuition is the highest in the United States. These credit services are used by the IRS, and financial information can be used to your company's detriment.

You will want to write Dun & Bradstreet and Lyons giving complete resumes on yourself, your management, and your directors, especially when you have hired strong outside directors, as recommended in this handbook. Additionally, you should give your tangible net worth in general terms (medium five figures) on an appraised basis, not historical cost, and so state it. Make any truthful, positive general statements you can, such as:

1. "Sales increased dramatically over the last year." (Even the money guys know the importance of sales to a small business.)
2. "Profits were earned."
3. "The last five years have been profitable."

4. "Strong profits have been earned since purchased by new owners."
5. "The backlog is presently 82 % over last year."
6. "A 57,000 square foot expansion is planned."
7. "Bank credit lines in medium five figures are presently not in use."

You can make some favorable credit comments about even the worst business short of "steady as she drifts". Close your letter with a statement to the effect that it continues to be your policy not to publish interim or annual financial statements.

Your commercial banker can also be extremely helpful in the establishment and preservation of credit. A letter similar to the one you sent to Dun & Bradstreet should be available to your banker. He can then edit it and send it out on bank stationery to vendors inquiring about credit with the understanding that your bank will send you a copy of their responses.

To better understand credit lingo, the following graphs might be enlightening:

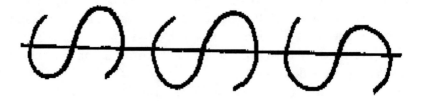

Line of Credit

Gross Margin

Chapter 25
The 'Price' of Success

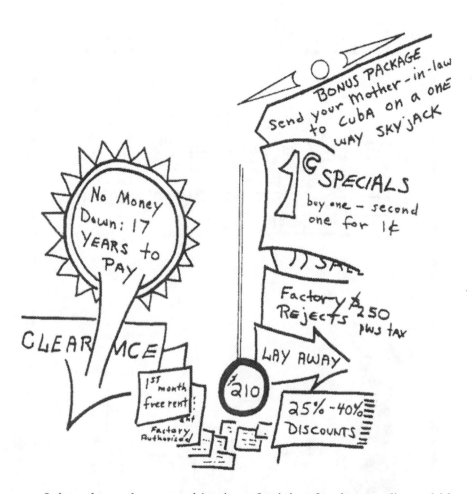

It has always been an objective of pricing for the supplier to kid the businessperson just as the retailer kids the customers. In effect, the purchaser thinks they are getting a bargain. Accordingly, it is not inappropriate to design your price structure to handle this situation, particularly when the "kid-ee" is a big customer.

It is worth reviewing your basic product to determine if it lends itself to accessories such as in the car industry. If it does (and it likely will), the accessory can be pitched in on a big order. What you want to insure is that your base prices remain intact and at the same time guarantees you an adequate rate of return so that you won't find at the end of the year that you've been knocking yourself out for nothing.

Another useful technique for manufacturers and distributors is to co-op advertising on larger orders. This is relatively cheap advertising that forces the customer to put equity in your advertising program by paying for a portion of the ad, usually half.

If you really want to be effective with your price list, announce to your customers well in advance of a price increase the fact that things will be going up and now is the hour to buy. To have their business in the future, you will want to caution that overbuying frequently results in a piling up of obsolete stock.

Since prices are so important in a modified capitalistic society, it is a worthwhile expense to neatly print your price list (even though it might change frequently) on a high-grade stock of paper. This even applies to price tags on the floor. The idea is to have the buyer remind himself that although prices might be steep, he is receiving an item of unusually high quality.

That violations by small businesses of the anti-trust laws in pricing will not be prosecuted is a myth. In particular, exchanging planned price lists with a competitor is by itself a violation of the Sherman Act. The consequences could be devastating - fines, imprisonment, treble damage actions and *parens patriae* suits by state attorneys general. Some seem surprised to learn that small businesses *can* be successfully prosecuted for "tying" arrangements, that is, the use of leverage over one product to force someone to buy or accept another product. A guitar and guitar case-maker forcing the guitar buyer to purchase the case is an example. The only thing worse than the anti-trust can of worms is trying to re-can the worms spilled and crawling away.

Above all, be bold with your prices. Price your goods or services as high as possible. Do not be timid. Your objective is to establish the highest price the market will bear, not just a reasonable mark-up from your cost. Remember, in a bad market you often cannot even get your cost, much less a reasonable mark-up from the cost. You can always come down in price, but going up after a price has been quoted or price list set can be construed as gouging.

Consumers, even seasoned buyers, sometimes equate high price with high quality, as marketing specialists are well aware; hence, you can sometimes up your quality through pricing without even an utterance of instruction to your quality control staff. The *Wall Street Journal* recently reported that a new mustard was packaged in a crockery jar. It flopped when the processor tried to sell it for 49 cents but turned into a gold mine when the price was changed to $2.90 a jar.

This melody also has another beat - fending off price increases from suppliers. Considerable skill is required, and the task should not be left to second-tier management. There are few who have the ability to stave off or postpone price increases. It is only natural to long to be loved, and you are going to make the vendor most unhappy if you are properly doing your job.

Strangely enough, many in second-tier management want love more than money particularly when it is not *their* money at stake. If you cannot get prices or increases in prices beaten back or reduced, postponement can save you a bundle. Watch out, though. Some vendors have few scruples in this situation and will try to get their desired price by reducing quality. If your quality control program really begins at the moment you receive your supplies, as it should, you can detect and thwart a reduction in quality straightaway.

Chapter 26
Getting There Indirectly

So, you want to have a job where you're the boss, the owner, the Head Honcho, the one who knows where the cheese is hidden. You'd like to dictate to yourself how you want this day to run and be the gal who makes all the decisions. The recipe calls for a dash of ego. Blend in some money. Advice is a necessary ingredient. Add bunches of luck. Stir well.

Franchising may be the road to your Pot 'O Gold. It is recommended over starting your own company since franchising is less risky. But, a franchise can be no better than the person who operates it. Hence, success is dependent upon you. What does the franchisee get? You pay a fee and in return receive an identity, a package of how-to-do-it management directives, a list of sources from which to buy the products you require and just about everything you need to know in order to run the business.

Why not do it yourself ? After all, there are many people who have not been happy with their franchise arrangements. Is franchising, then, a good way to go into your own business? There are two sides to the question. If you choose the franchise route, you give up part of your freedom of choice; running a franchise operation is not the same thing as being in business for yourself. What you are basically doing is buying yourself a job as a sort of a branch manager. Any respectable franchising licensor will demand that you follow orders and do it by the book. They quite often demand that you do your buying from the licensor. Quite a few franchising companies have encountered troubled waters because the franchisees have been unsettled by so many rules, regulations, and buying requirements that they no longer felt that they were in charge.

The negative side, then, is that when you buy a franchise you pay for a contract which immediately takes away part of that precious freedom which you had in mind when you first wanted to become an entrepreneur.

Now let's look at the other side.

The simple truth of the matter is that some independent businesspeople (retailers, service people, etc!) simply do not have the necessary organizational skills to successfully begin their own venture. They know only enough accounting to further confuse themselves. They don't know anything about control systems essentials to monitor the business. They don't know how to apply their time, steal watermelons, or joust with windmills. They know virtually nothing about how to find, interview, judge, and hire employees. They know nothing about federal and state regulations which determine tax matters and employment procedures.

In short, the entrepreneur without the necessary management skills, deficient in education, and lacking any experience at being his own boss will probably make too many mistakes, nudging even higher the mortality rate among new ventures. That's why it isn't so dumb to invest in a franchise. After all, the general idea among franchisors is to make their people successful. To accomplish that, they demand that you follow orders. Therefore, giving up part of your freedom, which is to say, the right to mismanage your own business, can be an equitable trade-off, one that can help you to avoid the pitfalls of starting your own enterprise.

You might say franchising is neither the fish nor fowl. You still buy a job, but your future and freedom is more limited to an independent business with unrestricted horizons. On the other hand, franchising can definitely circumvent the three to four years of loss you may well incur in starting your own business.

So, let's assume you've weighed all the factors and have decided to buy a franchise. If visions of wealth dance in your head when you review the myriad of franchises available, pause and exercise vigilance. To eliminate the possibility of creating a financial disaster, use the following checklist before you make your final decision:

1. Talk to at least three people who have purchased and are operating the type of franchise which interests you.
2. Obtain written proposals concerning your selected franchise territory. Leave nothing to chance. Seek a written, exclusive market.

3. Employ an attorney skilled in franchising to read over your agreement before you sign it. Make sure to do this *before* you part with any earnest money. If you don't know an attorney, ask your banker to recommend one. The legal fee is well worth it.

4. Using the same approach, engage a competent accountant. Don't ever plan to be in business for yourself without the help of this professional. Before you sign your franchise agreement and part with your money, seek his or her counsel. Assign to them the task of setting up your books of record.

5. Finally, check the business references of the franchisor. Ask the Better Business Bureau. Ask the local district attorney. Ask your exterminator if he ever dreams about bugs and roaches snuffing out his life. Better yet, ask the people who have done business with the franchisor. Don't worry about causing embarrassment. If the people are Mr. Clean, your investigation will be welcomed. It will be an endorsement of ethics which will produce new business. Otherwise, who cares about embarrassment?

In becoming a franchisee, take a few precautionary steps so as not to be a "rip-off-ee."

History of the Franchise Business

It has been suggested that the franchise industry is relatively new - that it has experienced phenomenal growth. It ain't necessarily so. Franchising dates back to just after the Civil War when Singer Sewing Machine Company began franchising dealers. The automotive industry is, however, the granddaddy of modern franchising. Automotive manufacturers needed rapid expansion manned by highly motivated owner-investors, not just salaried managers. Many other industries - oil, soft drink, fast food - have used franchising arrangements to expand their operations enormously in a short period of time with very little capital. Rather than being forced to sell and dilute capital stock, the individual franchisees provide the expansion capital. The franchisor's leverage is tremendous.

True enough, the franchising industry has grown extensively since World War II. But then, so has everything else. The growth is not exciting, phenomenal, or magical. Rather, it has been a steady, strong growth, a factor which any prospective investor in franchises should keep in mind.

The "Turnkey" Franchise

One word coined by the franchise business is "turnkey". The turnkey franchise is a complete business. The fast food franchisor, for example, locates the land, arranges to build the building, installs the equipment, and finds an investor to take over when it is ready to function. The investor then makes his payment, the date for opening is fixed, and the business is ready to go. With a turn of the key, he lifts off into the wonderful world of entrepreneurialism, kitchen grease pits, and dishes caked with slop.

I do not mean to suggest that the investor has been entirely left out of all the planning and development, but it is intended to point out that the franchisor might well select and utilize the services of an architect, a lawyer, a specialist in locating land, and in obtaining all zoning approval and all permits.

The franchisor has the operational knowledge of the particular industry and passes on this expertise to protect the investor from the gamble and guesswork of opening his own store alone. The investor will, at all times, be kept informed about what plans are being made and why and may even, in some decisions, be allowed to state his preference when there are options available.

The turnkey plan is expensive, requiring a significant amount of capital. For example, McDonald's requires a $430,000 to $750,000 start-up investment, most of which is for equipment, fixtures and signs. Included is an initial franchise fee of $45,000. The land is located and building built by McDonald's to specifications and leased to the franchise at a flat base rent, or, at least 8.5% of sales. In addition, McDonald's levies a 4 % monthly service cost on gross sales.

Another franchisor, Dunkin' Donuts, charges a one-time fee of $40,000 depending on site work done by the company. It gets a royalty of 5 % of sales.

AAMCO, the world's largest automotive transmission specialist, requires over $30,000 for the name and $197,700 to $222,400 for the investment. The real estate arrangement is similar to McDonald's. However, the 7 % royalty more than offsets the modest start-up cash.

The do-it-yourself franchise type, alternatively, is much easier to capitalize than a turnkey. For example, Baskin Robbins requires a franchise fee of $40,000 and royalties of 5 % to 6 %. Unlike a McDonald's, you simply build and lease the store and then buy the ice cream and supplies from Baskin Robbins.

Consider this further refinement on the do-it-yourself franchise: an accountant who has been working for another firm decides to enter business for himself. He buys a franchise from one of the nationally advertised tax preparation services. What does he get? Assuming he can show experience and competency, the franchisor will aid the accountant in training new employees for each upcoming tax session. The accountant is given access to home-office computers which print up a major portion of each income tax return. Necessary forms are available, and, of course, the nationally advertised name and reputation of the tax preparation service is further consideration for the fee.

Now, what is it that he does not get? What is it that he must do for himself? First, he must seek out and arrange for his own office location. He must employ his own people. The franchisor may assist a little bit, but, primarily, the task is left to the franchisee. Finally, no assistance will be given in choosing office machines, furniture or needed books and publications.

The accountant basically is paying a modest initial fee and a percentage of his yearly gross revenue for the privilege of using a nationally advertised name and known trademark or brand name.

Why does he buy this franchise? He believes that by buying a nationally advertised name he will attract more followers than the Pied Piper.

It's a do-it-yourself kind of franchise, and the buyer should understand that although franchise fees may be safe and reasonable, there remains much to do.

"Suede Shoe" Franchise Salesmen

Many franchisors hire, train and develop only top professionals to package, tout and sell their franchise. They carefully screen the type of people whom they employ, and they will not employ a high-pressure salesman of the type sometimes called a "suede shoe" boy. Other franchise companies definitely will and do employ these suede shoe flimflammers.

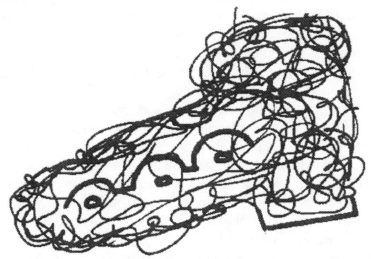

Suede Shoe Franchise Salesman

Please understand two things. First, the suede shoe salesman is probably working for a company with a weak franchise which is overpriced and understaffed. At the first sign of such high-pressure sales tactics, a neon sign in your brain should flash *caveat emptor*. Had you become a franchisee of Minnie Pearl Chicken Systems, Jerry Lewis Cinemas, Chips or Videorecord Corp., you would have lost your shirt by now. Franchisers have to file disclosure statements with the Federal Trade Commission and must provide a copy to a prospective franchise holder. Careful checking is the way to avoid a costly mistake. The failure rate of franchise outlets is small. While not comparable, that looks good alongside the fact that roughly 80 % of all new small businesses fail. Such high-pressure tactics have been hallmarks of fly-by-night franchise operators and should be a warning signal to you.

186

Second, suede shoe boys like to develop and use a variety of pitches, all high-pressure and all basically designed to convince the investor to sign on the dotted line right now. Tomorrow will be too late!

Here's how the dialogue might go:

Prospective Investor: "It is an interesting franchise and I may be ready to buy this plan, but first, I must discuss this with my lawyer and accountant".

Suede Shoe Salesman: "They don't know this business. Also, if you wait until tomorrow, it will be sold. We only have ONE for your area which will make you big profits with minimum effort."

"I am interested but I need to be in touch with some of your other nearby licensees to see how they came out. Is it possible for you to give me a list of some of them?

"Our company policy does not permit release of names of our licensees for reasons of privacy. Anyway, we have another substantial investor who has just committed, but I wanted to be fair to you since you reached us first."

"Let me have a week to think it over. Call me then."

"That week will cost you. We are adjusting our franchise fee price $2,000 Thursday."

Pay attention! You should know without even casting a glance downward that the fellow is wearing a flashy pair of suedes.

What's In a Name?

A corporate name and logo can be extremely helpful in establishing a good first impression and image in the customer's mind. We have agreed that the main advantage the franchisee gets is a recognized name whether turnkey or do-it-yourself. It is (dis)respectfully submitted that too little attention is paid to the name. Many franchises (and other businesses) used the founder's name, not always an intelligent tactic.

Many have succeeded in spite of a non-descript name, but more thoughtful consideration given to a name which would have created an indelible impression in the consumer's mind during their first encounter would have spared millions in advertising costs.

McDonald's? The name creates an image of a dirt farmer, naked from the waist up, plowing behind a work-worn mule stumbling over a chick-chick here and a chick-chick there. The name is household only because McDonald's was first. The company pounded the marketplace with billions of dollars of advertising over the years, and the memorable McDonald's "Golden Arches" logo created a lasting impression. AAMCO conjures up a bureaucratic image. Baskin Robbins sounds like the curse-word Hannibal uttered when he stepped in an elephant pie crossing the Alps. In addition, every time the franchise Snap-On- Tools is mentioned in a mixed group of slightly tipsy partygoers, all have to muffle their snickering.

To show you the indelible impression a name can "brand" on one's mind, Jack Smith of the *Los Angeles Times* reported on the publicity given to a certain cheese shop at the Art Center College in San Rafael. It was called Holy Cow. The logo which appeared on the storefront and on accessories, such as white shopping bags, was an "amiable-looking yellow cow with large see-through holes, like a piece of Swiss".

Also, the name Eyedeas was given to a purveyor of chic spectacles and sunglasses, Benjamin Franks to a hot dog chain, Back to Eden for a plant shop, Critters for a pet shop, Piece 'a Cake for a bakery shop and Once Upon a Time for an antique shop.

I thought of a few myself on the way to the bus station one day: Sew-it-Seams for a sewing shop, Nitwits for a knitting boutique, Pipe Dream for a tobacconist, and LBS, Ltd. for a weight-reducing spa. Not bad, Phil!

The idea is to remember to give thoughtful consideration to your brand name or trademark, whether picking it yourself or picking a franchise, and follow up with your name's registration with the patent office. Where possible the brand name should be a part of the corporate name or preferably the corporate name itself. Avoid using your surname lest the marketplace see you as something worse than a dirt farmer.

Now, after all this discussion, the big question on your mind, of course, is, "How much money does a franchisee make?" Can you make a good living at it? Yes, you can. The typical franchisee begins making money after the first year and can expect an 18 to 20 % pre-tax return on investment.

It's definitely worth taking that plunge. Just think of the veins pulsing in Goolsby's neck and the joy fluttering in your heart as you say your final goodbye.

Chapter 27
Promote to Strength

Sales are the lifeblood of any business, but the smaller the business, the more important sales become. Large businesses, as a rule, can cushion against the impact of sales softness, whereas a small business typically needs the funds generated by a sale to be immediately recycled.

Cash flow is essential. Accordingly, market planning is absolutely essential in your small business. You might slide by without overall company long-range planning and forecasting, but do not omit to formally prepare a market plan forecasting at least the next fiscal year's market goals, that is, where you want to be in your respective market(s) in terms of sales, growth expectations, and market share. Involve all spear-carriers in this important planning. Let them establish their own goals, and, as owner, you simply mesh these goals into a market plan.

You say, "Gee, my buddy made a wad in his business, and he never messed with a marketing plan". Well, I only say your buddy could have made more, perhaps much more, with a well-conceived marketing plan.

Rather than simply extrapolating your 7% compound growth rate to arrive at next year's sales, further delve into your sales focusing in on at least these areas:

1. *What is your present market position and what do you want your market position to be?*

You can never be everything to everybody even in big business. Since you cannot be one of the top three in ranking of market share for your product, your objective as a small business should be to locate yourself in a protected market position, and don't lose sight of what you are trying to do in the heat of battle – create a legal monopoly. To establish a protected market position, you might, as an example, be dominant in one geographic area such as being the leading retread tire firm in Kansas.

To carve out a niche, you might do customized work, concentrate on quick delivery, or make the only headache powder while the giants are producing only tablets. The newly emerging independent specialty retailers have each carved themselves a niche and continue to prosper against the large department store chains who are grabbing up the mass market at almost all price levels. While the chains are going down the middle avoiding specialized marketing approaches, a specialty store might continue to use their unique niche to get all the special business such as leather goods or electronics.

Of course, the chains can rarely offer personalized service. If you really think about it, truly great service is the *only* sustainable competitive advantage which cannot be leap-frogged. The independent retailer can place heavy emphasis on providing superior service. The idea here is to position yourself to have the lion's share of the market in your specialty so the customer will remember you when the particular need comes up. You might say you now have dominance in a market which you yourself have created. When the customer wants a grading firm specializing in building earthen dams, your firm, Damn Earthy Company, will come to mind.

2. *Which product has the highest markup and turnover and the most potential?*

Like your salespeople, you'll find 20 % of your product line is producing 80 % of your profit.

3. *What is your competition doing?*

I hesitate to mention this because many people get obsessed with their competitors to the point of distraction. However, your competitors do make up the market. They need to be monitored, and that can range from shopping the competition with a decoy to extracting information from independent delivery people or former employees stopping short, of course, of industrial espionage.

4. *How best to generate sales?*

Now that you know your competition, your market position, and the product lines with the most potential, you have to get the customers' interest through advertising, promotion, sales personnel, etc.

Here are three useful thoughts along these lines:

First, the typical small business should spend *more* advertising money, making sure the media and message zeros in on the targeted buyer.

Second, sales people should have the chance to be the highest paid in the company. To achieve this, compensation should increase per unit as sales increase: a 5% commission on the first $25,000, 6 % on the next $25,000, etc. Don't do as our curmudgeon Goolsby does and change the formula once you have one or two salespeople making more in commissions than you, the owner, make in salary.

Third, don't underestimate the power of people promotion. Think what Hugh Hefner, who is basically an introvert, has done for Playboy Enterprises with his showmanship. Malcolm Forbes generated more interest in the financial magazine bearing his name through widely ballyhooed promotions like being the first balloonist to successfully cross the United States in a single balloon and by opening his magnificent 50-room castle, Chateau de Balleroy in Normandy, to the public. Those cleverly orchestrated spectacles garnered more publicity than running multiple double-truck ads in *The New York Times.*

Consider that the class-B baseball club in my college days played to a packed house not because of the Durham Bulls' skill (I believe they finished seventh out of nine in the league) but because of the antics of Rufus Antionne, the third baseman. He was a 5' 1", lightning-fast, jet-black dynamo of a Frenchman who emitted a continuous stream of French (cuss?) words to the umpires while constantly darting around the infield, this much to the crowd's pleasure. He alone packed the ballpark. Unlike Michael Vick, Rufus Antione's substantial contribution to gate receipts generated by a desire by his fans to enjoy his showmanship on the field was not rewarded in those days with an nine figure, knockdown salary.

5. *How is the market receiving my product or service?*

This can best be learned firsthand by you, the owner, in direct sales. You should do this yourself from time to time. Witness Currier Piano Company. It had become an industry joke when its president hit the road at least one week a month attempting to sell both big shots and little shots. The laughing subsided after the company's sales increased 85% in a year when sales in the piano industry as a whole remained flat.

The marketplace cannot be studied merely by sitting behind a fat desk reading and having phone discussions with sales personnel. Tunnel vision sets in. The opportunity to make a detailed inspection of the quality of your product or service at the critical time just before the product passes to the buyer or consumer and not just before packaging at the factory, is important. The owner/manager needs to spend more time on the sales floor, at the lending desk, in the car lot, in the dealer's store and engaging in the art of one-on-one selling. In addition to gaining market information about mood and reception of your product, by actually selling, you re-learn the product, gain knowledge about it, and create goodwill.

This direct discussion approach is much more effective and substantially less costly than a $100 per person focus group. That is not to minimize new online consumer feedback services, which offer terrific advantages in that immediate feedback can be solicited about customers at a cost of pennies per opinion giver. That said, potential customers are much better at reacting to ideas than creating them, so personal involvement in your market certainly merits your valuable time.

Goodwill: The disposition of a pleased customer to return to the place where he has been well treated.

United States Supreme Court

Additionally, your personal batteries get re-charged, and you can become excited again over the benefits that your product or service gives to others. This renewed enthusiasm is highly infectious to all in your small business. Most importantly by far this is leadership by example at its best and shows the extreme importance of sales by doing, not just jawing. Without sales the other basic functions of business, such as finances, manufacturing, service, and the like are, at best, academic.

Like an outstanding trial lawyer, the professional salesperson knows that preparation, not a glad hand or a knee-slapping joke, is the secret to success. Winging it at a sales presentation insures failure. A salesman who doesn't know his customer's needs and background is about as helpless as a muzzled dog in a meat house. When the sales situation requires preparation, such as the sale of a life insurance policy, conscientious homework literally guarantees success.

Using the life insurance sale as an example, learn everything you can about the prospect. Don't focus just on the obvious, like where the prospect works, but inquire about such facts as their approximate worth and income, other life insurance policies they may own (asking this when setting up the interview is one way), their educational backgrounds, and likelihood of future wealth, such as from anticipated inheritances, and so on. Ask business associates if they know if a prospect is on the fast track to the top. Put yourself in the prospect's shoes. Anticipate questions or objections, including financial and tax consequences to the prospect that may arise from their financial situation. Now, are you getting the idea. Is preparation so unusual when you consider, for example, the planning and practice time before the Army-Navy game or the preparation and tune-up for the Masters' Golf Tournament?

The salesman, like the trial lawyer, is aided by quick mental reactions. Unlike the financial, credit, manufacturing, or purchasing people, he is on the firing line. Many sales hinge on having ready answers and responses, rather than going back and looking up an answer when new matter is introduced.

Do keep in mind in any sales-related endeavor the following admonition:

In one day,
Sampson slew
1,000 philistines
with the jawbone
of an ass.
Every day,
ten million sales
are killed
with the same
weapon

Chapter 28
The American Dream

Why should you want to be a small business owner?

Here are the major reasons why you should consider entrepreneurialism:

It is the great American dream! It insures job security inasmuch as you would not fire yourself.

The independence and freedom of ownership as well as the satisfaction of seeing the results of your decisions are highly desirable and provide further motivation for success.

With more and more people entering the job market holding college degrees, there will be a glut of management people. As a small business owner, you will avoid the rat race of the larger management pool and the hassle and headache of vying for jobs in large businesses.

The challenge of ownership is clearly a reason to become your own boss. The problems and challenges you will face along the way will sharpen and test your ingenuity.

From an economic point of view, small business ownership allows you to build an estate in addition to earning a salary. The company itself is an inflation hedge. Small business ownership affords you the same tax advantages available to the top management of larger businesses. And, of course, that long line to top management in the monoliths forms to the rear and is usually a quarter-century long. Why delay your satisfaction? Learn all you can from them and move on.

Here are some major things to consider before becoming a small business owner:

Search your soul. Do it long, and do it hard. Make sure your motive is truly born of a desire to become an entrepreneur and not to run away from an unhappy situation.

Take a careful inventory of your management talent to ascertain if you have the combination of grit, education, and applied management skills developed during a five-year (more or less) management internship with a large company.

Make sure you have considered the different lifestyles required of certain small businesses, especially the long hours demanded of new owners.

Make a detailed, written plan. In your plan, include the criteria you are looking for in your search for a going business to purchase. Include economic scenarios which you believe will unfold in the future. This will help you to purchase a business which can take advantage of expected growth. The 21st century holds a world of promise for those entrepreneurs willing to take advantage of exciting growth opportunities in new frontiers of science, technology, and service to humankind.

Consider purchasing a going concern. This will help you minimize the need for money - cold, hard cash by going against the grain and acquiring (usually by merely assuming debts, or, some of the debts) a business which is losing money because of inept management. You avoid the heavy start-up expenses of starting a new business from scratch.

You still will need money to operate your business. Small businesses have a seemingly insatiable appetite for money, usually for working capital to support expanding sales. A direct loan from the Small Business Administration is your best source. The interest rate is so low you are urged to borrow up to the statutory maximum and worry about what to do with the money later. Few of these loans are granted, however, because of limited federal funds for this program.

At this point, your versatile commercial banker becomes your best friend and money source. Even though banks have a number of better places to invest their money than in a small business, you can still get the loan if you develop the loan officer's friendship. You smother the banker with a mass of figures, statistics, projections, and analyses of your business. If you run into the rare situation of a bank with a qualified in-house financial analyst, who understands this mass of figures, quickly change banks!

A Small Business Administration guaranteed loan from a commercial bank is a third source of funds to consider. These are sweet deals for the banks. They get to charge the going interest rate even though up to 90% of the loan is backed by the federal government.

Your company will have excellent potential because it fits into all or most of the criteria you have established and is part of a potential growth market. Another reason the company will have potential is because you will be replacing its former inept management.

What will make your small business successful?

What must you do after you have acquired a going concern? How do you successfully function as a small business owner? Why is it that some entrepreneurs succeed while others fail? Successful owners spew profits out of their companies while the failures could not have made a bigger mess if they had dashed rotten avocados against the pavement.

Let's look at a number of characteristics and attributes of the successful *numero uno*. The successful entrepreneur always comes out on top, one way or the other, with ethics intact. Usually these people exercise leadership by example. They know that employees emulate deeds and actions. Words not backed up and committed by one's actions are hollow, signifying nothing. Accordingly, stoicism, ethics, humility, and a genuine concern for all employees are practiced by the owner who successfully sets a good example.

Organization is frequently buried by mission in the entrepreneur's mind. Accordingly, heavy emphasis must be placed on organization as the business prospers and grows. A Quick Read™ organizational chart with a brief job description on the chart by each management slot has been conceived and introduced by the author especially for small business (See Chapter 10). The chart shows at a glance where each management person fits into the company and what, in brief, the management person does. The chart is useful in understanding and planning. The selection and promoting of management people in this chart is critical.

The importance of hourly employees and their strong work ethic (needing only leadership) is greatly stressed. Avoid the two costly shortcomings of other companies (especially larger companies), that is:

1. The failure to inculcate full understanding and buy-in by employees at all levels on how the product or service benefits others; and

2. The failure to bake into all employees minds the corporate desiderata.

Albert Einstein said the Rule of 78's (explaining the power of compounding interest) was more startling to him than $E=MC^2$. Likewise, this author's epiphany in life was realizing the motivational power resident in an employee who understands and believes that what he or she is doing is really helping others. In our souls, all of us want to make a difference, help others, and help humankind. This motivates all to a higher level of profit achievement. The caveat, Dear Reader, is universal. Maybe the need to help others should also be given a rule number. Motivation of *all* people in the company is essential.

Various methods of communicating effectively both within the company and outside the company have been explored, with inexpensive audiovisuals getting the nod as the best method in most situations.

The dress of the business world is the conservative dark suit, white shirts, plain black socks, and traditional dark lace-up shoes. For "alpha" women, subdued stockings, the same dark suit, and a white silk blouse are the order of the day. For less formal businesses, conservative, understated, neat attire is the rule. Remember, "Thou shall not dress flashy now that thou art a successful owner."

Select outside professional people, such as your attorney, CPA, and financial and investment advisors, with great care and only after much thoughtful research. Experience and ability are highly important.

The giant web of government regulations and government harassment is far-and-away the biggest threat to the small business sector, and, unless corrected by each of us, could make small business go the way of the woolly mammoths. Anti-business tar pits are lethal.

The ability to digest information and current events in our fast-changing, internet world is essential to successful decision making. It is important to understand that the Industrial Revolution is at an end. We have entered the Age of Ideas. America is the world leader in idea creation. We are blessed and have a very promising future for our children and ourselves, for which we thank our ever watchful and benign Creator.

Being able to understand information about your own company and your vendors and customers through financial statements is essential. Accounting is the language of business and literacy is demanded. Remember also to be literate enough to protect your corporate privacy. "Eyes only" is a rule to be invoked before "baring all" (figuratively speaking...) on the Internet.

Finally, for every front-line dogface, ten support soldiers are needed. Even if all ten are military whizzes, the battle will still be lost if the front-line infantryman is a dud. Marketing is the infantryman of small business. Accordingly, the production and financial function is not given co-equal status with marketing.

Marketing is the working locomotive which pulls small business and gives it its momentum. Knowing small companies cannot compete with the substantially lower unit costs of the larger companies which dominate the market in their particular product, smalls *must* create a protected market niche in order to compete effectively with the behemoths.

A Final Word...

In the previous one hundred years, the nature of change itself has changed. Where before change moved at a turtle's pace, in our life times we have watched it accelerate to warp speed. The difference is palpable, and no one is immune.

The pace of business, and the new opportunities birthed by massive technological advances, has produced a maelstrom of new sales channels, new technology, new products, new and more efficient ways to compete, and great opportunity, all occurring in a "flat world" (For more on this subject, read *The World Is Flat – A Brief History of the Twenty-First Century*. By Thomas L. Friedman, Farrar, Straus and Giroux, April 5, 2005). The digital revolution continues to transform formerly backward, third-world countries into international, information-based economies. Witness India. With the help of a computer, Indian workers now process credit card transactions and answer your questions about how many frequent flyer miles you've used. Location is a non-factor in a global economy. Business can be transacted quickly and efficiently from anywhere in on earth and often at a cheaper cost.

Physical assets have become secondary to intellectual property. We are in the Age of Ideas. Companies that used to be moneymaking machines for decades no longer exist. Old business models have become obsolete. Change can now be measured in years, even months and weeks. Forget decades. The late author and economist Peter Drucker believed the most important policy was "to abandon yesterday". He was a man before his time. A book referenced in Chapter 21, "Attack and Die", teaches us yesterday is comfortable, and what used to work inspires hope that it will work again. Past success, however, is no longer a promise of future success in a rapidly changing world. Therefore, devote scarce resources to the future, not the past.

What does all of this mean for all of you aspiring entrepreneurs? In the new age of the globalization of business, "barriers to entry" are being destroyed; today an individual or company anywhere can collaborate with others or compete globally. Did you know that when you travel on JetBlue airlines, a homemaker in Utah, working part-time in her own business, might be making your reservation? How? She has an entrepreneurial spirit and a computer! The world, not just your town or your country, can be your "stage" and the platform from which you can start and operate your own successful, independent, and profitable small business.

It is hoped that the *logos* on how to become a small business owner and how to function as a small business owner, particularly leadership by example, will prove profitable. It certainly should! Like being born again, (remember, Nicodemus was a successful entrepreneur) small business ownership will set your soul soaring.

Opportunities abound for business start-ups in this new age. Now, boldly go out, fulfill your entrepreneurial dreams, and laugh your way to success!

Good night and goodbye, Mr. Goolsby, wherever you are!

Celebration after leaving Goolsby, as seen from inside beer cans…

REFERENCE ARTICLES FOR "SUCCESS IN SMALL BUSINESS IS A LAUGHING MATTER"

The Governance-Management DMZ:
Key to Effective Board-CEO Relations

By J. Phillips L. Johnston

Leadership is best put into practice when ambiguities of authority are eliminated—when responsibilities are clear. What is meant by governance and what is meant by management? The differences are considerable.

To assist in this process of creating an effective and productive relationship between the board and CEO, it is necessary to establish what I call the governance-management DMZ (demilitarized zone). Like its inspiration along the 38th Parallel separating North and South Korea—called by President Bill Clinton "the scariest place in the world"—the governance-management DMZ is an inviolable line into which no one dares cross. In this case, the DMZ prevents commingling and confusing board and CEO responsibilities. As with the no-man's-land that marks the boundary between the Koreas, board members and management venturing into this DMZ do so at their own peril. And, additionally, they put their companies at risk.

The governance-management DMZ serves two purposes. First, there is a clear understanding that the board is not to deal in administrative matters—not to micromanage. And, second, is an equally clear understanding that management is not to cross into new director appointments, Ends Policy, and other matters reserved for governors. If a transgression is made, unlike the DMZ at the 38th Parallel, neither group is subject to metal rain. A transgression, however, can jeopardize the ability to lead and work together collegially, which is critical for companies to grow market share and increase shareholder value.

Director Summary: Employing a "governance-management DMZ," or demilitarized zone, helps boards and management work together by: clarifying the roles of both parties, allowing more emphasis on vision, mission, disruptive strategies, and management execution where shareholder value can be augmented.

In short, establishing the governance-management DMZ assures that board members can lead effectively without undermining management's ability to run the business.

Don't Cross the DMZ: Shake Hands Over It

In the best-run companies, the DMZ is not the corporate equivalent of the Berlin Wall. Although it's strictly observed, the DMZ is more like a waist-high, split-rail fence. Directors and management are able to share information, materials, and provide mutual support. It's important to understand that governance-management is not an adversarial relationship. To be so would undermine the CEO and negate the very purpose of a board: to guide, support, and monitor. On the other hand, a board cannot be a rubber stamp. In the past two years, we've seen far too many examples of what can happen when boards merely serve as backslapping fraternities. There is a fine line between over-involvement and under-involvement. The best companies have it figured out. A clear understanding of areas of responsibility on both sides of the DMZ can help.

Specific Areas of Responsibility

The output of many boards resides permanently in an ends-policy notebook, which is unusually thin because ends policies, though broad, are succinct. Management's area of responsibility is means. It is no accident that means deliverables are lengthy, yet narrow in scope. Just compare an employee handbook with an ends-policy notebook.

This should come as no surprise. No one knows a company better than management. Management has superior day-to-day knowledge. This is understandable when you consider that, according to a 2001 NACD survey, the average board member prepared for and performed 190 hours of corporate board duties. Using an uncharacteristic 40-hour management workweek, managers, on the other hand, devote over 10 times that amount of time to their companies. Even though the board has

A unique and diverse view of the outside world is extremely valuable.

final responsibility for business plans and budgets, it is not a good use of time for the board to go into line-item inquiry. That's where the DMZ is invaluable, clearly delineating which responsibilities are governance and which are management:

- The board has the responsibility to develop policy; the CEO and management execute policies and plans.
- Boards deal with ends; management with means.
- Boards discern; management acts.
- Boards focus more externally; management looks more inward.
- Boards focus on the long term; management tends to be more concerned with the short term.
- Boards monitor; management manages.
- Boards establish a company's mission, vision, and values, codify them in writing, and monitor them over time. Management implements these policies throughout all corporate departments.

Mission, Vision, and Values

If boards should not go into line-item inquiry, what is their major function? The answer is mission, vision, and values. The board gives a broad outline as to how ethics must permeate, indeed, resonate throughout the organization. Management ensures values are inculcated and practiced. For the most part, boards have expertise in the world outside the company. That is why boards must become more diverse. Ethnicity is not just socially correct. A unique and diverse view of the outside world is extremely valuable to help envision where the corporate ship-of-state should navigate, on which rocky shoals its beacon should shine, and which sea lanes most likely lead to corporate growth.

Boards should reserve time to think through where the company should be and what it should look like as it continues to grow. These exchanges during board sessions play a strong role in helping the company successfully compete. Like the summer retreats in upper New York state in the 1870s, where people gathered to listen to and partake in intellectual discussions, these sessions can be thought of as "chautauquas." Most of these free-wheeling sessions do not produce ideas that grow into strategic programming. However, on more than one occasion, a board chautauqua has illuminated a new way of looking at programs, devised disruptive strategies, and led to added shareholder value.

Such success is directly attributable to an inviolable governance-management DMZ. Board chautauquas about mission, vision, and values, especially how these ethical components interface with the external world, are where boards bring the most value.

Personnel Responsibilities of the Board

Boards that cross the DMZ to deal in administrative and personnel matters dilute leadership so essential to directorship. To ensure the most effective and productive leadership, the board must have only one personnel responsibility: the chief executive officer. Some authors suggest that it is the board's duty to evaluate the performance of senior management, including their removal when necessary. Boards are not familiar enough with the day-to-day running of their companies to judge the competency of senior managers. Boards should not cross the DMZ to assume this responsibility. This is management's purview. The only possible exception is where there is an ethics issue that the board has an absolute fiduciary duty to address. Even then, the board's responsibility is carried out through the CEO. The issue itself should be corrected by management and on management's side of the DMZ.

Viewed from the bottom up, no corporate executive can serve two masters. The corporate board cannot be a helpmate to the CEO when it interferes in any way with line responsibilities. Moreover, a board member cannot judge management performance from the crow's nest of six meetings a year.

Conclusion

The age of the empowered board, catalyzed by the Sarbanes-Oxley Act (SOX), is fraught with danger. While SOX undoubtedly has much to recommend it, an overly liberal view of the Act can lead to an emboldened governance that SOX box-checks every responsibility under management's purview. Consequently, a strict understanding and separation of governance and management responsibilities must be observed. This governance-management DMZ is an idea that can and should become part of America's corporate structure. Companies will work more efficiently, effectively, and the result for many organizations will be an increase in shareholder value. To paraphrase Churchill, never will so many have owed so much to so few. ∎

J. Phillips L. Johnston, J.D., has served on the boards of five public and over 12 private companies, including 10 years of audit committee service for one NYSE-listed company. He also served as CEO for 10 venture-backed, primarily high-tech companies, including Digital Recorders, Inc. He is currently writing his third book, *Trust But Verify*.

The Pressing Need For Financial Literacy at the Board Level

By Phil Johnston

Can you imagine conducting business as a citizen of Rome without the ability to speak and understand Italian? Your problems would be obvious. Business success would be doubtful. Yet, in some respects, this very same situation is playing out every day in boardrooms across America. But here, the problem isn't language—it's numbers.

A recent study by the University of Chicago School of Management estimated that no more than 40 percent of public-company directors are familiar with the financial and accounting concepts necessary for them to be effective at their jobs. In particular, both the statements of cash flows and comparative and pro forma balance sheets are not well understood by some directors. Clearly, they should be. Both these statements frequently give more insight for strategic decision making than profit and loss statements.

Financial numbers are the language of business. Understanding what the numbers mean is essential at the board level. After all, directors are making multimillion-dollar decisions on the margin. Policy decision fiascos at the board level—those that cause stockholders and the business media to wonder, "What in the world were they thinking?"—often have financial illiteracy as their root cause.

The reason is clear. Some boards leave the "bean counting" to a few financial types serving on the audit committee. This is just asking for trouble. To be effective, each board member must understand the core business of the company he or she serves. Clearly, an understanding of financial statements and reports isn't something that board members can delegate. To fully understand the company, each board member—not just members of the audit committee—must understand the panoply of financial information affecting the company. By definition, excellent decision making depends on the entire board's understanding of what financial reports say about the business. If board members on committees other than the audit committee consider the company's financial ratios and statements to be indistinguishable from Egyptian hieroglyphics, the result will be the equivalent of a corporate train wreck.

Five Ways for Directors to Add Value

Boards have always had an absolute responsibility to oversee compliance, even before Sarbanes-Oxley accentuated this duty. In addition to the long-standing responsibility to *protect* shareholder value, boards also have major opportunities to *add* shareholder value. There are five primary ways in which boards add this value, and all require the ability to understand the financial numbers continually paraded before them. The five ways that directors add shareholder value are the cornerstones of a company's strategic policy:

- Mission
- Vision
- Values
- Mergers and acquisitions
- Succession (including CEO selection and change)

Mission and vision. A company's mission statement is designed to say precisely what the organization expects to achieve; vision concerns what the company wants to be when it grows up. A few companies, such as IBM and Digital Recorders, have tried to heighten the importance of vision by embracing a new word: desiderata. Like vision, desiderata means something needed and desired.

Mission must take into account corporate resources; vision policy is best discussed without

Director Summary: Directors will represent a much greater strategic advantage to their companies if they become financially literate. Oversight and planning in each strategic area: mission, vision, values, mergers and acquisitions, and succession planning, is enhanced by directors who understand the accompanying financial issues at a greater than superficial level.

the constraints of resources. Mission is best determined when it is thoroughly analyzed; vision is best when debated, as though the board was in Chautauqua, New York, in the 1870s, where philosophers, professors and forward thinkers debated ideas in the summer under shade trees. Even when there are no conclusions in the vision debate, it is meaningful to frame the issues. Participants should not be discouraged if the vision debate does not conclude with action items—most will not. Vision can take time to sort through. Consider how long it took Royal Dutch/Shell to see a world of opportunities beyond fossil fuel and to adopt a renewable energy policy. This sweeping initiative by Shell was based on financial analysis of all alternatives, as well as financial analysis of oil and gas as a commodity.

In analysis of mission, boards should drill down to the assumptions behind the corporate budget and how the mission ties to vision. It is unproductive, if not amateurish, for the board to visit corporate budgets line-item by line-item. Moreover, the board stands guilty of micromanaging as it crosses into management's budgetary domain.

The vision discussion should take place before the full board, and must be done frequently because of the increasing rapidity of changes in the marketplace. Vision usually adds the greatest shareholder value. The board's decision at United Parcel Service to become a logistics company, rather than a trucking company, is one of many examples.

Values. Value policy—and the process through which it is defined—brings life-giving oxygen to any company. Standards and behavior boundaries need to be seared into the company's culture at the board level. Even though the only financial consideration is a cost/benefit analysis of investing in, promoting, and inculcating a corporate-wide values program—including an ethics policy—value formulation can add greatly to a company's net worth, as evidenced at IBM, which lost $8 billion when Lou Gerstner arrived in 1993. He changed the culture from one of warring fiefdoms focused on selling mainframe computers to a more collaborative, performance-oriented approach selling service solutions. IBM earned $7 billion in 2001.

Mergers and acquisitions. Regarding M&A policy, studies have shown that more than half of all business acquisitions in the U.S. diminish shareholder value. The financial literacy of all board members, in both the purchased and acquired companies, is extremely important in order to seal a deal that actually benefits the new, combined company. The success of acquisitions is improved when boards establish and monitor integration considerations between the purchaser and the acquired. Integration policy should be front-and-center in any M&A policy discussion. Accordingly, the board will want to address how the target company fits into its vision policy. If the fit is truly synergistic, a price premium will be justified.

But, in order to get to that price, a certain financial acumen is required on the part of the entire board. After all, it's the entire board that votes on M&A, not just members of the audit committee. Another important consideration is the impact of M&A on the balance sheet. Again, this work requires the financial literacy of the entire board.

Succession planning. While not as financially intense as the other board methods to enhance shareholder value, succession planning is, nevertheless, essential to understanding the strengths and weaknesses of a company. Insightful succession planning is necessary for the board as a whole, and the compensation committee in particular, in order to profile and select a CEO who can successfully lead the company. Again, the board's financial literacy is critical when reviewing and testing a CEO candidate's accomplishments at previous companies against the candidate's proposal for compensation.

A Call for Action

This urgent call for financial literacy at the board level does not mean that directors should eat FASB for breakfast. But, at the very least, it should be mandatory that directors who lack the ability to fully understand financial statements and reports be required to enroll in and complete a college-level course in managerial accounting. Depending on the institution, the title of the course might be "Accounting Essentials for Corporate Directors: Enhancing Financial Integrity," and so forth. Such a course is designed for non-accountants. You don't even need to know that debits are "closest to the window." [Ed. Note: NACD offers an online course called "Scrutinizing Financial Statements" at www.nacdonline.org/seminars.]

Expected Results

Once a company's non-financial directors complete a course on managerial accounting, the quality of board decisions will improve, and the board will be more likely to have a direct impact on increasing shareholder value. In the end, a company's investment in each board member's financial literacy will be more than cost justified.

The only unexpected consequence of this call for boardroom financial literacy is that non-financial directors may actually find that bean counting is enjoyable. Entertaining, even. Then the secret will be out. Every new board member will want to be on the audit committee. Well ... one can always hope. ∎

J. Phillips L. Johnston, J.D., has served on the boards of five public and over 12 private companies, including 10 years on the audit committee of a NYSE-listed company. He also served as CEO for 10 venture-backed, primarily high-tech companies. www.phil@northstate.net.

V

The Capstone

"The ancient Romans had a tradition: whenever one of their engineers constructed an arch, as the capstone was hoisted into place, the engineer assumed accountability for his work in the most profound way possible: he stood under the arch."

~ Michael Armstrong ~
(Former CEO of AT&T and Hughes Electronics)

Visualize a corporation as an arch which requires a capstone at its apex to support the weight of expectations placed upon it. Director accountability is that capstone in the arch of corporate governance.

Accountability is unpleasant. It requires risk. Attempts to avoid accountability have chiseled away at the capstone and caused many a corporate governance arch to collapse. The lack of director accountability to shareholders is widely acknowledged as one of the root causes of many of the corporate scandals that have plagued our capital markets in recent years. When directors rate each other's governance capabilities through a peer review process, the arch remains strong and intact. Board members who are unwilling or unable to address deficiencies brought out in peer review should not be nominated for a successive term.

Peer review is not popular. The governance literature is rife with the protestations of the naysayers. Objections include:

- self-examination may be uncomfortable for some boards;
- collegiality among board members might be adversely affected, which could diminish the board's effectiveness;

---

¹ Jay W. Eisenhofer and Michael J. Barry, "Giving Substance to the Right to Vote [¶ 2.1]: The Need for a Majority Vote Standard," Corporation, LXXVII: 2 (January 17, 2006), 1-8

- directors might have insufficient knowledge of the contributions of other directors on the same board;
- reviews noting deficiencies on the part of one or more directors could become a lance in the hands of gladiator attorneys; and
- boards may perceive reviews as stern "grading" rather than improvement tools.

Based on my experience as a member of five company public boards and as CEO of two public companies, the value to shareholders of director peer review trumps all the objections. The absence of director accountability is nothing short of corporate hypocrisy. How can directors insist on accountability for others and invoke immunity for themselves?

A primary purpose of the Sarbanes-Oxley Act was to focus investor attention on the accountability of corporate boards of directors. A variety of prophylaxes have, since its enactment, been considered as possible building blocks for director accountability, among them direct nomination of directors by shareholders and election of directors by a majority vote rather than a plurality.

In 2003, Section 303A.09 of the NYSE Listed Company Manual adopted listing standards that encouraged boards of listed companies to conduct self-evaluations at least annually to determine whether the board and its committees are functioning effectively. NYSE companies' audit committees must do this. The real benefit of implementing such evaluations will be the long-term upgrading of director professionalism and downgrading of what has been called the "male, pale, stale buddy system".

Peer review serves many constructive purposes, key among them being improvement of director performance. Peer review is primarily used to identify performance shortcomings so that corrective measures can be taken. In the final analysis, the nominating committee must take the results of peer review into account in determining whether to nominate a director for a successive term. Self-evaluations by each director and evaluations by each director of overall board performance have their place, but director peer review is the gold standard and gets immediately to the heart of accountability.

Director peer reviews must be overseen by competent, independent third parties, preferably with board experience, armed with evaluation templates adapted to reflect the uniqueness of each board, and possessing the discipline to follow-up and address any identified deficiencies. Frequently, business attorneys with requisite experience perform this function because they know how to preserve evidentiary privileges and how to handle records retention issues so as to minimize accessibility to sensitive director critiques. Boards should only conduct their own peer reviews if they are prepared to referee disputes that may erupt, and to expose their most sensitive internal discussions in the media and courtroom.

Peer reviews must be conducted in confidence and be anonymous. No director's name should be attributed to any comments. Collegiality is one of the hallmarks of a successful board. Follow-up is absolutely critical to the process. The board must commit to reviewing the results of the evaluation and be dedicated to addressing the issues that it raises. An analogy can be drawn to employee handbooks. Essential as such a handbook

---

[2] Robert L. Hedrick and Dayton Ogden, "Board Independence: Striking the right Balance," Director's Monthly 30:2 January, 2006), 1-5

may be to employee relations, it is far better not to have published one at all than for the employer to adopt one and fail to follow its procedures. So it is with peer review, where the stakes often are magnified.

Meaningful director peer review and the accountability it engenders place the capstone in the corporate governance arch. It can have the single greatest impact upon board performance. If a board wants to do one thing to improve corporate governance, let it do this one, important thing. Insist on director peer review or risk the collapse of the arch.

J. Phillips L. Johnston, J.D.
http://www.Web2ohTV.com

Reprinted with permission from the National Association of Corporate Directors (NACD) May 2006 issue.

STRATEGIC CORPORATE BOARD MINUTES

Under Delaware law, as in other states, a corporation's business and affairs "shall be managed by and under the direction of a board of directors." A written record of the board's decisions, in the form of minutes of meetings and written consents to action taken without meeting, are required by law. There is advice in the legal literature that supports a "minimalist" approach to the preparation of minutes. As Sophocles observed, "No enemy is worse than bad advice".

WHY MINUTES

• Shareholders and directors meetings are required at least annually under state law. Failure to comply and to document compliance through appropriate minutes is one factor courts have considered in denying the limited liability protection of corporate status.

• Minutes provide a record of important corporate transactions. A "paper trail" can be important if disputes arise. It can demonstrate to shareholders, creditors, the IRS and the courts that the company and board acted appropriately and in compliance with applicable legal requirements.

• Directors sometimes approve business transactions in which a director has a conflict of interest. Properly drafted minutes can help prevent legal problems by documenting that those decisions were made, after full disclosure of the conflict of interest and in compliance with the procedure prescribed by law.

• Banks, trusts, escrow and title companies, property management companies, and other institutions require corporations to provide board and/or shareholder resolutions approving transactions, such as loans, purchases, or rental of property. Potential buyers of a company will ask to review the minutes of shareholders and directors of the company to be acquired.

• Auditors review minutes of all board, committee, and shareholders meetings.

• The new Form 8-K reporting requirements mandate reporting of all matters to be disclosed within four business days. Board action may be the triggering event for disclosure, and review of board minutes by the compliance personnel of a public company allows the timely determination that an event requiring disclosure has occurred.

• Best corporate governance practices encourage prompt preparation of minutes.

PROCEDURAL MATTERS

A procedural checklist for board and committee meetings should be maintained.

• Notice of the meeting, a preliminary agenda, and director reference material should be sent in sufficient time before a meeting to afford directors an opportunity to consider the items and reference materials before the meeting. A copy of the notice should be placed in the minute book. The agenda can be incorporated into the minutes by reference.

• The presence of a quorum and the approval of the prior meeting's minutes should be noted in the minutes. A scrivener with knowledge of the business who is skilled in the complexities of corporate governance should be designated to act as secretary of the meeting and assigned the task of taking the minutes.

SUBSTANTIVE MATTERS

- Minutes should reflect that appropriate corporate governance *processes* were observed. In matters in which the business judgment rule may come into play, minutes should document that the directors adhered to the standards required to invoke it.

- The more important a matter is, the more detailed the minutes with respect to it should be. This does not mean minutes should be a virtual transcript. It is normally neither necessary nor advisable to note who said what. The objective is to document the processes and outcomes.

- Whether documents should be incorporated by reference in, or attached to, minutes requires careful consideration. Material evidencing the processes by which the board reached a decision on matters of substantial importance should normally be included.

- Motions and votes should be accurately recorded in the minutes, including votes in opposition to a motion and abstentions.

- Conflicts of interest on the part any director should be disclosed promptly. Strict compliance with the processes provided under governing law is then required. Even though governing law may not so require, it is recommended that a director who has a conflict withdraw from the meeting after making full disclosure of it, and remain absent while the matter is discussed and the vote taken.

- Adjournment must be by motion and vote. It is important that both be recorded in the minutes.

- A draft of the minutes should be prepared by the secretary promptly after the meeting and forwarded to the chairperson for review and comment. The draft should then be sent to all directors for any corrections, absent which the minutes should then be signed by the secretary and the chairperson.

- Approval of the minutes by the Board at a subsequent meeting constitutes those minutes as the official record of what transpired at that meeting. In order to insure the accuracy of those minutes, before approval, each director should thoroughly review the proposed minutes and compare them with any notes from the meeting that the director prepared. Once approved, each director should discard his of her notes from the meeting as the director will be bound by the content of the minutes which are approved.

COMMITTEE STRUCTURES

In-person attendance at meetings should be strongly encouraged. When it is not practical for some of the directors, the remainder of them should meet in person and conference the others on land lines or by video.

A board or committee meeting that is otherwise duly convened in which some or all directors participate by telephone constitutes a legal meeting. Such telephonic meetings are adequate under certain circumstances, such as, a follow-up meeting, or a meeting to resolve issues of relatively minor importance, and are sometimes necessary in emergency situations. However, they are not preferred. A face to face meeting provides the greatest opportunity for an open and frank discussion of the matters before the body.

The above recommendations are not applicable to meetings under new § 303A.03 of the NYSE Listed Company Manual, which mandates "regularly scheduled executive sessions without management." These executive sessions - commonly called lead director meetings - are useful for public companies as a forum for discussion. Action cannot be taken at them unless, in an emergency situation, the board delegates such power. Moreover, CEO performance and CEO succession-planning are center stage, and these meetings should only take place in a face-to-face setting. Lead director meetings are a best practice and are strongly recommended for not-for-profit companies where public trust is all-important. The agenda is best kept brief and the minutes need *only* state that the meeting took place, name the non-management directors attending and incorporate the agenda by reference.

BUSINESS LAWYERS AS SCRIVENERS

- Do not underestimate the importance of the business lawyer in the process of reviewing drafts of minutes. Lawyers and others not steeped in corporate governance can miss nuances such as:

    - Preservation of attorney-client privilege - Recess a regular meeting and convene a separate meeting when counsel gives legal advice. Keep privileged minutes of the separate meeting.

    - At the point of insolvency, directors owe *creditors* a fiduciary obligation.

    - Appropriate content of the record of certain critical processes such as M&A considerations or CEO-hiring and terminations is important.

On one hand, corporate minutes are not a verbatim account of a board's proceedings nor should they be. By definition they are a summary of what occurred during a meeting. On the other hand, minimalism in recording minutes, though long-advocated and reinforced by tradition, is not a correct nor desired approach. Because it is difficult to hold directors individually and collectively accountable when decision-making processes are either not in place or ignored, *process minutes* encourage a higher level of accountability, and, when properly drafted, protect both the board and shareholders.

NEW MATTERS

Enclosed is the article dealing with the unique governance issues of an emerging technology company.

- Chief Creative Officer (CCO) rather than CEO for emerging technology company.

- Profile of CCO vs CEO with the requirement that CCO needs to be steeped in the technology.

- The CCO's role in crossing the classic technology chasm Godfrey Moore conceptualized.

- How directors of the emerging company must "slot down" into a limited management role on occasions.

- Smart venture capitalists should be Advisory rather than statutory board members.

I believe you will share in the belief that these "new matters" will add to the business knowledge base.

Phil Johnston, J.D.

EFFECTIVE BOARD LEADERSHIP
OF THE EMERGING TECHNOLOGY COMPANY

The role of directors of an emerging start-up technology company is far afield from that of directors of a mature company - in some instances almost dichotomous. To effectively steer an emerging company through the Gibraltar straits of start-up requires a special crew with a very specific skill set. Experienced board members of mature companies, especially CEOs and former CEOs of large companies, can be abject disasters as directors of start-up technology companies. In fact, the more successful the CEO of the large company, the greater the peril to the emerging company and its board. A start-up may appear to have all the attributes of a successful large company. To the former CEO it looks like a duck. It walks like a duck. But this emergent duck is most definitely a duck out of water!

Crossing the Chasm:
How the Roles of Large Versus Emerging Company CEO's Diverge

Emerging companies, like children, go through various stages of growth before they reach puberty and then maturity. Emerging companies, typically, are started by a highly motivated entrepreneur. She has conceptualized the technology and business idea, formulated the plan for market entry, overseen the early growth of the business, brought stability to the company's expanding operations and generally set the future growth agenda. Typically, the board would designate this founder a CEO, but, in the case of an emerging company, a more descriptive title might be CCO (for Chief Creative Officer). The small company will undergo many permutations over time. The founder could do well in the early stages, but flounder as the company crosses the chasm into the mass market, heads up an IPO, or deals with more people reports. Roles change rapidly for all in a high-octane growth environment, especially that of the founder.

Hence, the board would initially designate the founder as the CCO. The CCO function superimposed upon Godfrey Moore's classic graph will be a useful:

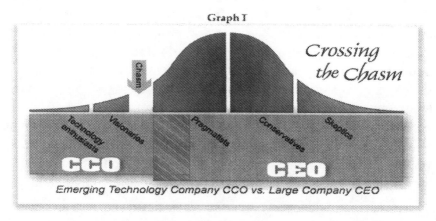

Graph I

Crossing the Chasm

Emerging Technology Company CCO vs. Large Company CEO

A fluid title such as CCO recognizes the attributes of a successful emerging technology *Numero Uno,* namely, her ability to decide the trade-offs necessary to developing a new technology, the ability to work with directors in "slotting down". This is a technique by which a director moves into a temporary execution role at the management level. Directors might agree to slot down to do the following management functions: negotiate a bank loan or deal directly with a vendor, work hands-on to get the company on it's feet, solicit initial investors, add early adopters as customers and guide the company across the all important chasm to mass market appeal.

The CCO of an emerging company will secure the early adopters at the outset of the graph and then initiate sales to the first "pragmatist" in the mass market. The expertise of the large company CEO, in contrast, has proven skill in addressing the mass market, that is, the bulge on the graph after the chasm. The large company has no need for a director to slot down. To the contrary, at large companies, a figurative de-militarized zone (DMZ) between the board and management makes slotting down unworkable. Such companies have depth of management with executives who neither need nor appreciate being micro-managed.

In mature companies, the successful CEO has extraordinary delegation and people skills, comprehension of financial statements, decision implication to those financials and the important big company mantra of *actual-versus-budget-management.* The CEO's success over the years reinforces these disciplines and carries over into everything, including corporate governance. Like a one suffering from syphilis, this can lead to blindness. A start-up has a long journey to the point where skills like *budget-versus-actual* become useful disciplines. An emerging company has no budget initially. It is in a rapid growth phase and traditionally relies on venture capital for its funding. The following graph aptly illustrates for directors the dichotomy of skill sets between the large and small company CEO/CCO:

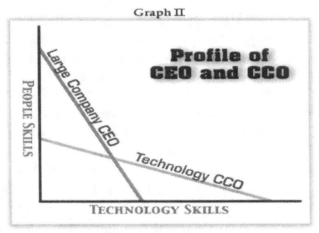

Before I took Digital Recorders public, it was decided to bring a Fortune 100 C.E.O. on our board. The new board member was, and still is, considered to be, one of the best large company C.E.O.'s in America. He took a huge tobacco company to the "next level". He understood how to inject blue dye into the veins of a company that had achieved maturity. But, it became apparent almost from day one that his *budget vs. actual,* big company approach was an impediment to an emerging, high-growth technology company. The budget he conceived for us was obsolete the moment it was published. So was his career as a director of our company, perhaps his first rejection in a successful career when we failed to re-nominate him to our board.

If the large company CEO serves an emerging company, their most valuable contribution will be to help shape the company's goals and vision and serve as a mentor to the CCO. A CEO has the experience to be an effective mentor, but other CEO proficiencies will not become useful until critical mass nears. Jeff Emmult, the current CEO of GE, needs only people and financing skills and the discipline of *actual-versus-budget* to lead. These skill sets are not as critical to growing a high tech company.

The skills needed during technology start-up will be weighted toward technical versus people skills for obvious reasons. This is a frantic, research-intensive, capital-raising, "beat the bushes" time in the life of the company. People skills are important, lest the CCO run off all his investors and partners, but technical skills are essential for business success. The CCO, by necessity, needs to have technology proficiency. A large tech company CEO, on the other hand, requires few technical skills. Her company has crossed the chasm to mass-market appeal. Moreover, there is a fully staffed engineering or PhD. researcher division. Energy must be focused on maintaining and growing market share which is best accomplished by nurturing the mission and vision of the company.

Board Characteristics of the Emerging Company

In her article "How To Seat A Solid Board" *(EETimes,* Monday, June 27, 2005), Lori Wirbel writes, "Entrepreneurs pulling together their first start-up often try to emulate the qualities they see in large public companies' boards when assembling their own. Some traits are indeed universal: Boards should be a mix of company management, investors and interested outsiders... And the directors should work within the general Sarbanes-Oxley rules of corporate accountability... since established governance practices are good policy for any company, public or private." However, that is where the similarity to large company boards ends.

Size matters. The number of directors should be limited to five or so. Large company boards have many more directors. Because most start-ups require access to large amounts of capital, venture firms investing in the start-up typically have the first "dibs" on board seats. Venture capitalists understand the uniqueness of an emerging technology company and pack a world of experience. However, they have an inherent conflict because they have a primary duty to their fund. Venture capitalists routinely bow out as board members on IPO day.

Independent directors, who should share the vision of the CCO, play a crucial role perhaps introducing additional funding sources as well as bringing a fresh perspective and unbiased insight to issues. They should be well acquainted with the emerging company's industry and have knowledge of the company's technology and target market. Having a "rolodex" of industry contacts is an added bonus. Outside directors of large companies, in contrast, are often from outside that company's industry entirely. The potential for conflicts of interest in the form of lack of objective oversight could become a significant problem for venture capitalists on the board. Hence, in the interests of good governance it is recommended that venture capitalists serve on an advisory board rather than on the statutory board. The troublesome conflict with duties as a venture capitalist is thereby resolved and the legal liabilities of the statutory board are minimized. After all, venture capitalists have ample control and power as major shareholders of the start-up.

Although Sarbanes-Oxley (SOX) is not applicable, the emerging company should adopt SOX best practices in the initial stage. Director knowledge of the underlying business and its financials is important. SOX requires directors to take an active role. Directors come to meetings prepared. Like board directors, venture capitalists must limit their advisory board service so as not to be overextended. Pedigree, so important in the boom years of the 1990's, is all but irrelevant. Expertise and preparedness have replaced "hype".

Large boards must embrace diversity in selecting its members. The wide human spectrum that is today's brutally hypercompetitive global marketplace must be represented on the modern board. Large corporate boards must employ these human tools to effectively compete. A start-up is, of course, limited in that regard by the small size of its board. Diversity for diversity's sake should not be the rule. However, if a qualified candidate can bring both diversity and knowledge to the board, a progressive board will nominate that person to serve.

Functions of the CCO and Board of Directors of the Emerging Company

The contribution of a thoughtfully assembled board to the success of an emerging company can be enormous.

"Slotting Down"

Along the growth continuum, the role of the lead entrepreneur undergoes an on-going and dramatic metamorphosis. In the early stages, much energy is focused on achieving short-term goals, such as securing facilities, assembling a management team and attracting and serving initial customers. Once the board is in place, it may be called upon to jump into the fray and help out with some of these responsibilities. This is called "slotting down": moving from the more traditional board functions such as setting strategic policy (articulating a company's mission, vision and values) to actually getting some dirt under its figurative fingernails and doing nitty-gritty grassroots work alongside senior management. Unlike governance of large companies with "nose in - hands out", the board sticks its nose and *both hands in.* One of the most important of the functions a director might perform when slotting down is raising money, especially doing so with a very short fuse. A start-up's ability to raise funds is limited. Directors may contribute their own funds or use their personal network of friends and business associates as investors.

The "DMZ"

It should be understood, however, that this "slotting down" is a temporary situation, not the norm. It is a dangerous precedent indeed for a board to venture into the management woods and set up camp. The DMZ, that line between the authority of the board and that of management, should be inviolate except in the case of ethics violations or moral turpitude. The success of a company over the long haul hinges upon trust and the board and management clearly understanding its functions and responsibilities. As the company grows and matures, the need to cross the DMZ ends. The board articulates direction. Management implements it. Now both hands come out. But, the nose *always* stays in. Here's why: In practice, the DMZ is more like a waist high, split-rail fence. Directors and management are able to share information, materials and provide mutual support. The directors need to be in the information "loop". This is not an adversarial relationship. Otherwise, the very purpose of the board - to guide, support, and monitor the CEO - would be undermined. On the other hand, in this age of Sarbanes-Oxley and its strict new oversight requirements, the board must be careful not to be a rubber stamp.

Mentoring and Explicit Vision - The Key to Emerging Company Success

In a successful emerging company, the role of the CCO and the board will continually evolve. A CCO with technology proficiency and little management experience will not, however, morph into a butterfly without help. In his insightful article "The Role of the Board of Directors in the Successful Start-Up of New Ventures", Dr. Michael S. Camp notes that in the early growth stage, "though the process can be difficult, most entrepreneurs understand that the single greatest threat to the future growth of the business is their inability or unwillingness to delegate as their role changes.

(MacMillan, 1983)... The goal of this phase of the start-up process is to stabilize operations so that management can shift its focus away from market entry issues [such as crossing the chasm] and begin to develop a more long-term perspective for the young venture." Both the CCO and the board should take active roles in this evolutionary process.

Camp then turns his attention to the future growth of a company: "Though marketing and financial issues have dominated the entrepreneurial team's attention to this point, they now begin to consider growth issues and the need to reformulate their vision for the future." This involves increasing the "opportunity mindset" of key managers and *declaring innovation as a basic building block of the future."* Andy Grooves and the Intel board bet the ranch when they developed and introduced the microprocessor, which "ate" their storage chip babies. This revolutionary new technology turned disruptive strategy changed the rules of engagement in the microelectronic marketplace, making Intel a figurative computer nation.

Interestingly, studies of emerging companies have demonstrated a strong correlation between innovation consistent with a company's ability to formalize their mission and vision over time and the company's continued strong growth. In a study conducted by Mitsuko Hirata of Tokai University in Kanagawa, Japan and reported in her research article "Start-up Teams and Organizational Growth In Japanese Venture Firms", Ms. Hirata found that successful companies "adapted to change more easily", demonstrated a "greater degree of adaptability and flexibility, which ultimately meant that their start-up team could evolve into a management team", "kept discussions open and were not afraid of conflict", and, most importantly, "had a different approach to organizational growth by *utilizing an explicit vision "* from which they did not stray. The company's culture was formed by "imprinting an entrepreneurial spirit" from the outset, enabling it to first shape and then sustain that vision. These characteristics were key in the company's continued growth, enabling them to successfully cross the chasm. This spotlights the notion that a free and open exchange of ideas is exceedingly important. Emerging companies benefit greatly from board initiated and inspired competitive ideas, even those coming out of left field, if they can be discussed without a boardroom meltdown to reach consensus. This sort of disruptive strategy at the board level can revolutionize the board's relationship to the company because it focuses beyond any known horizon in search of new solutions and better ways of doing business. The process involves not only management but harnesses the imagination of every employee in inventing new ways of doing business by creating new business models before the marketplace invalidates the current ones. The competition is disrupted in a way that enhances and creates shareholder value. This approach to new business strategies is uniquely suited to emerging growth companies.

After finally crossing the chasm, emerging companies should then go on to capture and retain majority market share and build a moat around the technology market they now dominate.

Summary

The dichotomy between the roles of directors in large versus emerging technology companies may be summarized by the following:

	Emerging Technology Company	**Mature/Large Company**
Likelihood of success of large company CEO as	Very low; perhaps zero.	High.
Size of board and board mix matter.	Five directors, 1 CCO; 2 or so VCs. 2 independent directors. Aim for diversity, but	7-12 directors, 1 CEO and one CFO with balance of directors being outsiders.

Attributes outside board members must have.	Understand technology and tradeoffs. Experience in crossing the chasm in technology marketing. Industry	Eats financial statements for breakfast. Experienced and proven strategic thinker. Aptitude
Do homework in advance of meeting and attend	Always be prepared and on time. Expect monthly meetings.	Always be prepared and on time. Expect 5-6 meetings per year.
strategically is where company's process and policy level add shareholder value.	boards, maximum. Must have ability and willingness to "slot down".	maximum 4 other boards, period. Never slot down; never cross DMZ, but need to be partner with management.
Build a knowledge base.	As independent director, essential that she knows industry. A bonus to be part of that industry. Helps greatly to have industry rolodex.	Big premium on ability to think strategically. Still must learn company's core business and industry.
The loyal opposition should be just	Board members are free to have different beliefs and policies	Never cross DMZ. Be collegial but
Need for director to "slot down" and do	Frequently necessary to "slot down" to stand side-by-side with	Industry outsiders welcomed as directors. Essential to
Independent Directors and Venture	Conflicts of interest abound with VCs. Solution is to provide	Independence rarely an issue except directors can fail

Successful big company CEOs are not the best choice as directors of emerging technology companies. The unique nature of director responsibilities of an emerging technology company are foreign to these titans of industry whose prior successes tend to render them blind to the unique traits required as a director of an emerging company. Directors of emerging companies together with the CCO need unique skills different from those of large company boards.

The most important director skills in an emerging technology company are mentoring senior management, utilizing the techniques of "slotting down", which means crossing the "DMZ" when necessary to meeting growth objectives, and, determining strategy to cross the chasm from the early adopter to the mass market. If an emerging technology company has vaulted the chasm to mass-market appeal, one can be sure it has capitalized on the skills of a thoughtfully assembled board that understands and has practiced these disciplines.

By always refreshing and renewing its vision, an emerging company board can transform itself and its young corporate protege from a pre-market ugly duckling to a post-chasm swan. The most successful emerging companies are those who gave shape and form to an explicit vision from the outset. They continually build their corporate culture and core competencies around that vision, inspire loyalty to it, re-define and give it new expression as the company grows. This is key in a rapidly changing, dynamic business environment where success is spelled I-N-N-O-V-A-T-I-O-N.

Graphics by:
James E. Woody, Graphic Artist
... design... illustration... photography..
1401 Woodsman Court
High Point, NC 27265
Phone: 336-869-3440
Mobile: 336-848-1165
email: jjbtwoody@yahoo.com

Male, pale and stale

Too many corporate boards persist in denying seats to women and minorities.

BY J. PHILLIPS L. JOHNSTON

I N 1963, IN THE SHADOW of the Lincoln Memorial in Washington, D.C., a young man gave one of history's most famous speeches. The man spoke for an entire race of people who, since their arrival on these shores more than 200 years earlier, had been denied equality in almost every aspect of American life. The man was passionate and eloquent. Most memorably, he spoke of a dream for his children and for his people. Five years later, after being vilified in the national media, spat on, bruised by water cannon, attacked by police dogs, jailed, and threatened with death, the man was assassinated.

Today, much of the man's dream has come true, yet much remains to be done. In no place is this truer than in the corporate boardroom.

It's appropriate to evoke the memory of the Rev. Dr. Martin Luther King Jr., for we can't speak of diversity, multiculturalism, or minority opportunity — in any industry — without acknowledging Dr. King's seminal role in laying the groundwork upon which the dream was built. Our country has come far in 40 years; yet were he alive today, Dr. King would not be sat-

J. Phillips L. Johnston has served on five public company boards and has been CEO of a number of venture-backed technology company turnarounds. He was chief executive of Digital Recorders Inc. prior to becoming special counsel to the law firm of Nexsen Pruet Adams Kleemeier in its Greensboro, N.C., office. He has also been the chief government regulator of North Carolina's $18 billion credit union industry. He is the author of two books, including *Success in Small Business is a Laughing Matter*, which *Esquire* magazine called "the best book ever written about small business."

isfied. And, frankly, neither should the chairmen of America's corporate boardrooms.

A corporate shame

Although strides continue to be made to diversify America's corporate work force — and the supervisors, managers, and directors who oversee it — the corporate boardroom remains overwhelmingly white and male. In October 2003, women and other minorities made up 51% of the employed American work force. However, 10% of all directors at S&P 1500 companies are women and 8.8% are minorities, according to the Investor Responsibility Research Center in Washington. There is even less diversity in the boardrooms of smaller public firms. This is a corporate shame. It is indefensible. And, even more to the point, at the midpoint of the first decade of the 21st century, this shortsightedness borders on abrogation of the board's fiduciary responsibility.

In all "Business 101" courses, whether at a small, public college or at Harvard or the University of Chicago, students learn the same lesson on the first day of class: *The goal of the company is to increase shareholder value.* Period. Although you'd never know it from recent headlines, it is assumed that this goal is both pursued and achieved ... legally. That this is not always the case is yet another, even more eloquent argument for diversity in the boardroom.

Because the board leads the company in matters of corporate mission, vision, and values, the board has the same goal as the company: an increase in shareholder value. But by not even attempting to represent the vast human spectrum that is today's global marketplace — a marketplace that is brutally hypercompetitive and does not suffer fools — corporate boards are denying themselves the depth and breadth of associative knowledge and are denying their companies the human tools with which to effectively compete. This *should* be a textbook case of corporate malfeasance. That it is not is proof of the inbred, cliquish, and virtually accountability-proof nature of the corporate boardroom.

This assertion is neither pandering to a "special interest" nor hyperbole. It is simply fact. And it should be obvious. Consider:

• Bureau of Labor Statistics data confirm that the fastest-growing segments of the U.S. population are Hispanics and African Americans.

• More nuclear families' major breadwinners — if not decision-makers — are female.

• The fastest-growing overseas markets for American products during the next several decades will likely be Chinese and Mexican.

The boat needs rocking

White male board members helped make the USA No. 1, so why rock the boat? The boat has changed. At one point in our history the clipper ship dominated the commercial sea lanes between America and Great Britain. Today, the clipper ship is a romantic relic of a bygone age. Just as the clipper ship evolved into the steamship, which, in turn, evolved into the behemoths that currently ply the world's oceans, the face of the American work force has changed, is changing, and will continue to change at an increasing rate. The corporate boardroom must keep pace. Here's why.

Most public company directors see the outside world in the same way. Their paradigms are virtually identical. Most board members had middle-class or upper-class childhoods, just like me. Most are male, pale and stale: the product of private schools, just like me. Most are highly educated: CEOs, MBAs, and J.D.'s, just like me. Most think less government is better and most believe in self-reliance, all just like me. You have to study *The Autobiography of Malcolm X*, *The Nine Nations of North America*, and *Zen and the Art of Motorcycle Maintenance* to understand just how one-dimensional the white male view of the world is. Again, just like mine. If the function of the board is to provide guidance in corporate mission, vision, and values, the vision most white male board members are likely to provide is monochromatic. Monochromatic vision in a world of increasingly vibrant colors is a recipe for stagnation, if not abject failure.

No, this isn't tokenism

It should be very clear that what I am talking about is *not* tokenism. No woman or minority should be placed on any board because "it's the right thing to do." To say there are no women or minorities who can bring intelligence, experience, and ultimate value to a board is idiocy, if not abject sexism and racism.

Women and minorities are elected to a board for the very value and experience they bring to the table. It is through their eyes that boards can see, arguably for the first time, the new opportunities that America's growing diversity affords. It should also be clear that this opportunity benefits the *entire* company and all the company's shareholders, not just the employees or shareholders who happen to share the new board member's race or sex.

Because white males continue to monopolize the

What the boards of the Fortune 100 look like

Board demographics by race and gender

Fortune 100	Total Seats	% of Total Seats
Public Company Boards	1,195	100%
All Males	993	83.10%
All Females	202	16.90
Total Minorities	178	14.88
Total Females and All Minorities	344	28.79
White Males	851	71.21
White Females	166	13.89
Total White Males and Females	1,017	85.10
Minority Males	142	11.88
Minority Females	36	3.01
Total Minority Males and Females	178	14.90
African-American Males	93	7.78
African-American Females	27	2.26
Total African-Americans	120	10.04
Asian-American Males	9	0.75
Asian-American Females	3	0.25
Total Asian-Americans	12	1.00
Hispanic Males	40	3.35
Hispanic Females	6	0.50
Total Hispanics	46	3.85

Source: The Executive Leadership Council, *2004 Census of African American Directors on Boards of Directors of Fortune 500 Companies* (www.elcinfo.com).

boardroom, they tend to treat diversity as a social issue rather than the economic issue that it truly is. According to a white paper by Business for Social Responsibility, minorities and women contribute more than $1.5 trillion annually to the U.S. economy. Clearly, a compelling argument can be made that a diverse board is as much an economic imperative as it is a social responsibility.

Compelling benefits

What are the specific competitive benefits that result from a diverse board, and what is the evidence that a diverse board results in increasing shareholder value? Although little direct research has been conducted to gauge this relationship, it seems clear that the well-known benefits of a diverse *work force* should transfer directly to the boardroom. After all, the board has ultimate responsibility for guiding the leaders of the work force. According to the aforementioned white paper, research from Fortune 500 companies shows that a diverse staff enhances financial performance, reduces turnover, improves productivity, increases job satisfaction and employee morale, decreases vulnerability to legal challenges, and enhances the corporate reputation. Anecdotal evidence exists that diverse boards bring with them these same advantages.

> No woman or minority should be placed on any board because 'it's the right thing to do.'

Carl Guardino, president and CEO of the Silicon Valley Manufacturing Group — a consortium representing 125 companies — said in an interview with the *Palo Alto Weekly*, "Increasing boardroom diversity is essential to compete in a diverse international market ... With our types of industry, it is really a global enterprise, and we need to compete with every niche. You don't do that as well without different perspectives, and having women and minorities on your boards provides that." In the same article, Judy Hamilton, president and CEO of FirstFloor Software in Mountain View, Calif., agreed: "As a company you're saying to your employees, 'This is an open society and theoretically you can make it to the top.' That's probably the most important reason in my mind."

My personal experience with two dozen public and private boards mirrors this view. None of these boards were diverse except for Digital Recorders Inc., a Nasdaq-traded company, which has had two women, an Asian, and an African American as board members in its 20-year history. The company's strategic policymaking since the 1994 IPO, due at least in part to diverse governance, has helped make Digital Recorders a high-octane company that has captured majority market share in transit electronic destination signs and voice announcements. Because of its governance, and the diversity built into its governance, Digital Recorders is more competitive than the other four public companies and more than a dozen private companies on whose boards I have served.

Muddled mission, myopic vision

The true purpose and value of the corporate board is in providing the company with mission, vision, and values. Everything a board *should* do emanates from these three functions. And of these three functions, vision is the most important. When boards discuss what the company wants to be when it grows up, they are executing vision. Vision should be the subject of intense discussion. It should be a continuing agenda item.

Without a diverse board to focus these discussions, a company's mission can become muddled, its vision myopic, and its values questionable at best. For the past two years, even a cursory reading of the newspapers makes all too clear the *worst* that can happen to corporate values. More specifically, there is virtually no chance that any board will produce meaningful "ends policy" without minorities to expand and focus the debate over mission, vision, and values. This is also true in other areas of governance, especially in employment policies and ethics.

Time for new blood

Dr. King once spoke of the jobs that provided economic opportunity for millions of African Americans and other people of color in the 1960s. He said, "If you are called to be a street sweeper, sweep streets even as Michelangelo painted, or Beethoven composed music, or Shakespeare wrote poetry. Sweep streets so well that all the hosts of heaven and earth will pause to say, here lived a great street sweeper who did his job well."

Dr. King's words were reflective of his time. Today, in our time, it is well past the hour when the words *street sweeper* were replaced by the words *corporate board member*. It is time for some who are male, pale, and stale to step aside for new blood, especially women and minorities with unique viewpoints. The continuing vitality and global dominance of American business depend on it. ∎

The author can be contacted at pjohnston@npaklaw.com.

Economic Benefit of Diversity in the Boardroom

In 1963, in the shadow of the Lincoln Memorial in Washington, D.C., a young man gave one of history's most famous speeches. The man spoke for an entire race of people who, since their arrival on these shores over 200 years earlier, had been denied equality in almost every aspect of American life. The man was passionate, eloquent, and, most memorably, spoke of a dream for his children and for his people. Five years later, after being vilified in the national media, spat on, bruised by water cannon, attacked by police dogs, jailed, and threatened with death, the man was assassinated.

Today, much of the man's dream has come true. And, today, much remains to be done. In no place is this truer than in the corporate boardroom.

An Indefensible Corporate Shame
It's appropriate to evoke the memory of The Reverend Dr. Martin Luther King, Jr., for we can't speak of diversity, multiculturalism, or minority opportunity in *any* industry, without acknowledging Dr. King's seminal role in laying the groundwork upon which the dream was built. Our country has come far in 40 years; yet, were he alive today, Dr. King would not be satisfied. And, frankly, neither should the chairmen of America's corporate boardrooms.

Although strides continue to be made to diversify America's corporate workforce – and the supervisors, managers, and directors who manage this workforce – the overwhelmingly white, male nature of the corporate boardroom continues to give ground grudgingly. In October, 2003, women and other minorities made up 51% of the employed American workforce. However, 10% of all directors are women and 8.8% are minorities that hold seats at S&P 1500 companies according to the Investor Responsibility Research Center in Washington. Smaller public firms have more dismal with even less diversity. This is a corporate shame. It is indefensible. And, even more to the point, as we approach the midpoint of the first decade of the 21st Century, this shortsightedness borders on abrogation of the board's fiduciary responsibility.

Whether "Business 101" is taught at a small, public college with no national reputation, or at Harvard or University of Chicago, students learn the same phrase on the first day of class: *the goal of the company is to increase shareholder value*. Period. *The goal of the company is to increase shareholder value*. Say it again and commit it to memory. *The goal of the company is to increase shareholder value*. Although you'd never know it from recent headlines, it is assumed that this goal is both pursued and achieved ... legally. That this is not always the case is yet another, even more eloquent, argument for diversity in the boardroom. But, more on this later.

Because the board leads the company with sage wisdom on corporate mission, vision, and values, the board has the same goal as the company: an increase in shareholder value. However, by not even attempting to represent the vast human spectrum that is today's global marketplace – a marketplace that is brutally hyper-competitive and does not suffer fools – corporate boards are denying themselves the depth and breadth of associative knowledge through which they lead, and, by definition, are denying their companies the human tools with which to effectively compete. This *should* be a textbook case of corporate malfeasance. That it is not, is proof of the inbred, cliquish, and virtually accountability-proof nature of the corporate boardroom.

This assertion is neither pandering nor hyperbole. It is simply fact. And it should be obvious. Consider that 1) Bureau of Labor Statistics data confirm that the fastest growing segments of the U.S. population are Hispanics and African Americans, 2) the nuclear family's major breadwinner – if not decision maker – is increasingly female, and 3) foreign markets for American products and services that will grow fastest during the next several decades will likely be Chinese and Mexican. Given this well-researched data, the $64,000 question becomes clear. If a significant portion of your retirement funds are invested in *Acme Homebuilders* (apologies to Wylie E. Coyote), would you be comfortable knowing that Acme's board of directors look like a reunion of "My Three Sons" at Augusta National?

I thought not. Neither would I.

White Male Board Members Helped Make the USA #1 – Why Rock the Boat?
The boat has changed. At one point in our history the Clipper Ship dominated the commercial sea lanes between America and Great Britain. Today, the Clipper Ship is a romantic relic of a bygone age. Just as the Clipper Ship evolved into the steamship, which, in turn, evolved into the behemoths that presently ply the world's oceans, the face of the American workforce has changed, is changing, and will continue to change at an increasing rate. The corporate boardroom must keep pace. Here's why.

Most board members of public companies see the outside world in the same way. Their paradigms are virtually identical. Most board members had middle-class or upper-class childhoods, just like me. Most are white, male, and the product of private schools, just like me. Most are highly educated: CEOs, MBAs, and JDs, just like me. Most think less government is better and most believe in self-reliance, all just like me. You have to study "The Autobiography of Malcolm X", "Nine nations of North America", and "Zen and the Art of Motorcycle Maintenance" to understand just how one-dimensional the white male view of the world is. Again, just like mine. If the function of the board is to provide guidance in corporate mission, vision, and values, the vision most white male board members are increasingly likely to provide is monochromatic. Monochromatic vision in a world of increasingly vibrant colors is a recipe for stagnation, if not abject failure.

No, This Isn't Tokenism
It should be very clear that what I am talking about is *not* tokenism. No minority should be placed on any board because "it's the right thing to do." To say there are no minorities who can bring intelligence, experience, and ultimate value to a board is idiocy, if not abject racism and sexism. Minorities are elected to a board for the very

value and experience they bring to the table. It is through the eyes of minorities that boards can see, arguably, for the first time, the new opportunities that America's growing diversity affords. It should also be clear that this opportunity benefits the *entire* company and all the company's shareholders, not just the employees or shareholders who happen to share the minority board member's race or sex.

In my experience, some boards have, in fact, tried to bring diversity to their conference tables by electing a labor union delegate to represent members of the union. This is not only wrongheaded, it is dangerous. Electing a board member to represent only a segment of the company, or part of the shareholders, guarantees immediate friction at the board level, decreasing leadership value to corporate officers, and, ultimately, failure in the marketplace.

"It's an *Economic* Issue ... Stupid!"

Because white males continue to monopolize the boardroom, they tend to treat diversity as a social issue rather than the economic issue that it truly is. According to a White Paper by Business for Social Responsibility, minorities and women contribute more than $1.5 trillion annually to the U.S. economy. Clearly, a compelling argument can be made that a diverse board is as much an economic imperative as it is a social responsibility.

What are the specific competitive benefits that result from a diverse board, and what is the evidence that a diverse board results in increasing shareholder value? Although little direct research has been conducted to gauge this relationship, it seems clear that the well-known benefits of a diverse *workforce* should transfer directly to the boardroom. After all, the boardroom has ultimate responsibility for guiding the leaders of the workforce. The aforementioned White Paper by Business for Social Responsibility concludes that research from Fortune 500 companies shows that a diverse workforce enhances financial performance, reduces turnover, improves productivity, increases job satisfaction and employee morale, decreases vulnerability to legal challenges, and enhances the corporate reputation. Anecdotal evidence exists that diverse *boards* bring with them these same advantages.

In a 1998 online edition of Palo Alto Weekly, Carl Guardino, president and CEO of the Silicon Valley Manufacturing Group, a consortium representing 125 companies, said, "Increasing boardroom diversity is essential to compete in a diverse international market ... With our types of industry, it is really a global enterprise, and we need to compete with every niche. You don't do that as well without different perspectives, and having women and minorities on your boards provides that."

In the same online article, Judy Hamilton, president and CEO of FirstFloor Software in Mountain View, agrees, saying, "As a company you're saying to your employees, 'This is an open society and theoretically you can make it to the top.' That's probably the most important reason in my mind."

Increased competitiveness is a clear catalyst for increasing shareholder value. In a recent issue of *The New Zealand Herald*, Karen Price, a law firm partner and president of the Auckland Women Lawyers' Association, said, "While there is no way of judging whether board diversity helps keep companies ethically on track, there is evidence from U.S. research that it does help company competitiveness. It's associated with greater receptivity to change and to higher levels of creativity and innovation, because board members are more likely to offer and challenge different points of view."

My own, personal experience with two-dozen public and private boards mirrors this view. None of these boards were diverse except for Digital Recorders, Inc. (TBUS: NASDAQ). Digital Recorders has had two women, an Asian, and an African American in its 20-year history. The company's strategic policymaking since the 1994 IPO, due at least in part to diverse governance, has helped make Digital Recorders a high-octane company that has captured majority market share in transit electronic destination signs and voice announcements. Because of its governance, and the diversity built into its governance, Digital Recorders is more competitive than the other four public companies and over one dozen private companies on whose boards I have served.

Muddled Mission, *Myopic* Vision, and *Questionable* Values

The true purpose and value of the corporate board is in providing the company with mission, vision, and values. Everything a board *should* do emanates from these three functions. And of these three functions, vision is the most important. When boards discuss what the company wants to be when it grows up, they are executing vision. Vision should be the subject of intense discussion, like the thrilling intellectual give-and-take that occurred in Chautauqua, New York during summers in the late 1800s. Vision should be a continuing agenda item.

Without a diverse board to focus these discussions, a company's mission can become muddled, its vision myopic, and its values questionable, at best. For the past two years, even a cursory reading of the newspapers makes all too clear the *worst* that can happen to corporate values.

More specifically, there is virtually no chance of producing meaningful Ends Policy for any board without minorities to expand and focus the debate over mission, vision, and values. This is also true in other areas of governance especially in employment policies and ethics.

Conclusion

Dr. King once spoke of the jobs that provided economic opportunity for millions of African Americans and other People of Color in the 1960s. He said, "If you are called to be a street sweeper, sweep streets even as Michelangelo painted, or Beethoven composed music, or Shakespeare wrote poetry. Sweep streets so well that all the hosts of heaven and earth will pause to say, here lived a great street sweeper who did his job well."

Dr. King's words were reflective of his time. Today, in our time, it is well past the hour when the words *street sweeper* were replaced by the words *corporate board member.* The continuing vitality and global dominance of American business depends on it.

####

Section 304(1),
The Whistleblower Provision:
The Real Power Behind Sarbanes-Oxley

By: J. Phillips L. Johnston, J.D.

Abstract

Shooting The Messenger

For centuries, it's been an unwritten tenet of war that one side does not shoot the other side's messenger. The respectful treatment afforded messengers plying their trade back and forth between enemy lines, has been codified in great works of literature. In Henry V, Shakespeare has young Henry receiving the French messenger several times before the gruesome battle at Agincourt in 1415. Each time, the messenger faithfully and dispassionately relays the French King's rebukes, insults, and demands for surrender. And, each time, Henry contains his rage, knowing the herald is merely repeating what the king told him to say. Just before the battle begins, Henry listens to the messenger deliver the last of the king's insults, then sends him away with these words: "Herald, save thou thy labour; Come thou no more for ransom, gentle herald ..." If only Shakespeare were writing for 21st Century corporate CEOs.

Until recently, 'shooting the messenger' was an accepted practice in corporate America, albeit figuratively. With few exceptions, whistleblowers could expect to be ostracized, demoted, transferred, and, more often than not, fired. The impact on the families of whistleblowers was tragic. Of course, that was by design. The implication was that if you wanted to keep your job, if you wanted to stay in the game, you had to play ball. Or, at the very least, obfuscate, ignore, and deny the fouls committed by your own team. This shameful treatment of people who only wanted to do the right thing, caught the attention of mainstream America in 1999, when Hollywood released "The Insider," starring Russell Crowe.

The Sarbanes-Oxley Act of 2002

In the summer of 2002, President Bush signed his name on a piece of paper and the Sarbanes-Oxley Act became the law of the land. The official purpose of Sarbanes-Oxley, or SARBOX, as some refer to it, is "An Act to protect investors by improving the accuracy and reliability of corporate disclosures made pursuant to the securities laws, and for other purposes."

The most well known provisions of SARBOX are 1) both CEO and CFO must certify quarterly, in writing, that their financials are correct, and 2) if the financials are not correct, "I wasn't aware" no longer works as a defense for a disengaged CEO and CFO. Criminal penalties will apply. Of course the idea here is that when a CEO and CFO are required to actually sign on the dotted line that everything is on the up-and-up, checked, and re-checked *so help me God*, the scandals ascribed to Enron, WorldCom, Adelphia, et al., can be avoided.

SARBOX Section 304(1): Whistleblower

Clearly, it is a major step forward to have CEOs and CFOs now 'guarantee' that their financials are in order, and, by implication, that they aren't squandering corporate dollars on $20 million Van Gogh's for their beach homes. However, I believe a powerful argument can be made that the most far-reaching impact of SARBOX lies not with the autographs of CEOs and CFOs on a dotted line, but with the 44-words contained in Section 304(1). "Each audit committee shall establish procedures for the receipt, retention, and treatment of complaints received by the issuer regarding accounting, internal accounting controls, or auditing matters; and the confidential anonymous submission by employees of the issuer of concerns regarding questionable accounting or auditing matters."

Welcome to 'whistleblower'! This section of SARBOX will prove to be the real change agent and the most lasting legacy of the act. For while nefarious CEOs and CFOs can always *try* to make an end-run on SARBOX, they can no longer shoot the messenger who brings their nefariousness to light. The cost-benefit of the whistleblower provision is so favorable that private companies, not subject to the legislation, will also be swept up in this freedom-from-retribution tsunami.

Whistleblower Effects on Employees

Very simply, the reign of terror perpetrated against corporate employees because of information they share regarding corporate malfeasance, has ended. This is good news. The only people who don't view this as good news are executives with something to hide. Corporate fraud – malfeasance of any kind – can, and has, destroyed dreams and disrupted hundreds of thousands, if not millions, of innocent lives.

The wording, "confidential anonymous submissions," in Section 304(1) of SARBOX, prevents management involvement in the whistleblower process in any way. Clearly, the process must be kept out of the hands of management to circumvent a potentially unresponsive or resistant bureaucracy. And, of course, there is always the concern of management involvement in a process where management is implicated. Not unlike putting a fox in charge of security for the henhouse. By vesting responsibility in the audit committee, and ensuring confidential anonymous submissions, the process will encourage complainants to come forward. It will also erase the fear that complaints will be suppressed or the complainant will be the object of retaliation.

Any effort that guarantees an avenue of redress without recrimination is a giant step forward. The whistleblower provision of SARBOX gives us this step forward.

Whistleblower Effects on Boards of Directors

The Whistleblower provision, with its direct tie-in to a board's audit committee, is as strong an opportunity to strengthen the board as an independent counterweight to management, as I have seen in my 38 years as CEO of 10 venture-backed companies and director of 5 public and 15 private companies. The SARBOX whistleblower provision provides value to corporate boards in three ways:

1.   An early warning system to catch potential problems in time to prevent or mitigate the effect of misconduct and the resulting liability.

When I was Administrator of the $18 billion credit union industry in North Carolina, insider tips to my office uncovered over half the defalcations. Our audit staff uncovered the others. However, in most of the cases uncovered by the audit staff, too much time had elapsed between the start of the crime and its discovery. In most cases, meaningful restitution was simply not possible.

2.   A catalyst to heighten ethics.

Whistleblower will elevate both transparency and ethics. Like Neighborhood Watch, in a community concerned about safety, quality of life, and property values, it will soon be apparent that no bad deed goes unnoticed and unpunished. Whistleblower will link the act, and its consequences, so strongly, that potential perpetrators will be dissuaded from acts that, previously, had a better than average chance of success.

3.   The opportunity to enhance a company's reputation boosts public trust and enhances net worth.

When evidence of corporate malfeasance was filtered up through company management, as it typically was prior to SARBOX, the results were less than gratifying. In most cases, the effort was a waste of time and, as shown earlier, led to a complete implosion of the whistleblower's life. The whistleblower provision of SARBOX now provides an opportunity to gain unbiased information for better management decisions and board policy. Information reported confidentially and anonymously through an independent third party, such as an audit committee, is unvarnished and rapid. Untainted information will also elevate strategic decision making at the management and board level where multimillion-dollar decisions on the margin are made. Interestingly enough, the comic strip "Dilbert" frequently captures how information passed up the ranks to management is tainted by self-interest.

Whistleblower Effects on Shareholders

The SARBOX whistleblower provision will also have a significant impact on maintaining shareholder value:

1.   It encourages the discovery of malfeasance at an early stage.

Since the first investor bought the first share of stock, there has been a direct relationship between corporate news and the price of its stock: good news usually prompts an increase in stock value and bad news has the opposite effect. Catching malfeasance at an early stage, while not the greatest news, is certainly better than catching it so late that a company finds it impossible to repair its reputation.

Typically, it rarely does any good for a forensic audit to catch fraud more than a year after its initiation. The perpetrators have either spent their ill-gotten gains or safely hidden it in offshore accounts. Often, as we have recently seen, public outcry is such that the company cannot survive. The effect of protecting confidential and anonymous whistleblower call-ins will help catch malfeasance at an early stage and, thereby, protect shareholder value.

2.   The opportunity to discover fraud perpetrated by extended constituencies.

Vendors, customers, shareholders, banks, analysts, and stock exchange officials will be encouraged to use confidential, secure 800 numbers and encrypted, anonymous E-mails. Whistleblower makes it much easier for an employee of a shipping vendor to do the right thing when he overhears a loading dock supervisor encourage workers to short pounds on a textile company's shipments. When this fraud is brought to light early in the illegality, both the textile company's profitability and shareholder value can be preserved.

3.   Uncontaminated and timely information facilitates both management and board-level decision making.

Corporate profitability and shareholder value both depend on uncontaminated and timely information getting to the board. The whistleblower provision of SARBOX encourages the efficient and effective dissemination of information crucial to corporate viability.

Whistleblower Will Be Embraced Beyond SARBOX

As the benefits of early and uncontaminated whistleblower information to board audit committees become obvious, public companies will encourage new constituencies to share relevant information regarding fraud. As mentioned above, vendors, customers, shareholders, banks, analysts, and stock exchange officials will be encouraged to use confidential, secure 800 numbers and anonymous E-mails. In the case of vendors, an anonymous tip that a supplier is cutting corners on shipping could save the user company millions of dollars.

Private companies will immediately embrace the Whistleblower concept with open arms. School systems will pony up. Government agencies and not-for-profits will see advantages. Even though these organizations are not subject to SARBOX, the cost-benefit will be compelling. Even if defalcations and sexual harassment were the only issues, savings would be substantial.

The Downside of Whistleblower

There will always be disgruntled employees, with no legitimate complaint, who use Whistleblower as a means for their own, personal retribution. This is going to happen. However, expert, independent services with attorneys trained in information collection, retention, and distillation, will give professional guidance to audit committees. Legal guidance is of crucial importance. After all, the audit committee is comprised of independent board members whose work for the board is part-time. They have jobs outside the company on whose board they sit. By legal definition, and the spirit of the original legislation, the audit committee cannot turn to management for help. Recently, both Coca-Cola and Denny's embarrassed themselves by posting information on their corporate websites that requested employees report auditing and accounting wrongdoing to "senior management."

Some pundits may say that the whistleblower process is *too* good. It may unearth facts regarding situations best left hidden; exposing the company, its officers, and directors to liability. This is absolutely groundless. Among experienced board members, it is fully understood that the sooner one learns of a problem, the easier and less costly it is to resolve.

The third seeming downside of the whistleblower provision of SARBOX is Big Brother. Even though George Orwell was describing the government in his classic book, 1984, some will see the whistleblower provision as encouraging too little privacy and sharing too much transparency. Hogwash! The elevation of corporate ethics beyond a written ethics policy, as well as the very favorable cost-benefit relationship, clearly trumps this concern.

Implementation of Whistleblower is Proving a Challenge

Even though common and statute laws provide anonymity and confidentiality to a complainant reporting to a company's Ombudsman (up to the point of potential loss of life), employees' knowledge of, and experience with, companies that monitor phone calls and E-mails contaminates this process. Case law, in time, will corroborate this. Company counsel, alter egos of management, cannot oversee the whistleblower process. Outside auditors, even though they technically work for the audit committee, have the appearance of toting water for management. This subverts confidentiality and anonymity. In point of fact, outside auditors are weaved into the fabric of management on a daily basis.

The Value of Independent Service Firms

Public companies can fully comply with SARBOX section 304(1) by engaging outside, independent firms with secure 800 numbers, the ability to receive anonymous whistleblower E-mails, and a proven way to guarantee "retention and treatment of complaints." Service firms with expertise in advising corporate boards will provide substantial added value in overseeing this process and, after analyzing the data collected, interacting with the audit committee. When directed by the audit committee the vetting and analysis by the professional service firm will be invaluable information for independent auditors to identify and assess risks. Lawyers with expertise in corporate law and the collection and distillation of information, will dominate these specialty service firms. Again, audit committee members have substantial duties outside the companies on whose boards they sit. The biggest corporate sin, in my opinion, is half-baked information at the board level.

Summary

When properly implemented, Sarbanes-Oxley section 304(1), the whistleblower provision, not only safeguards, but substantially benefits, shareholders. When this process is thought out, adopted as policy, and executed at the board level, there will be a clear benefit to the corporation's bottom line. Public companies will voluntarily extend the whistleblower system to various constituencies in addition to mandated employees. Even those private companies not covered by SARBOX, including schools, government agencies, and not-for-profits, will embrace the whistleblower provision once its bottom-line benefits are fully appreciated.

In the 15th Century, Henry V clearly understood that a good king, a smart king, a king with his subjects' best interests at heart, does not shoot a messenger who brings him bad news. To the contrary, such a messenger is treated well. He's done the king a service. Today, in the 21st Century, corporate CEOs will come to the same conclusion in time, and with a little help from the whistleblower provision of Sarbanes-Oxley.

Phil Johnston has served on 15 private and 5 public boards, including 10 years of service on the audit committee of a NYSE - listed company. He has been a CFO, & a CEO of ten venture backed, primarily technology companies, 2 of them public, and has served as chief government regulator of the $18 billion N.C. credit union industry. Phil is a frequently nationally published author and lecturer on corporate governance, he is also the author of two books, including one that Esquire magazine called the "the best book ever written about small business". He is currently writing a new book entitled "Disruptive Strategy at the Board Level". He graduated from UNC Law School, attended the Stern MBA School at NYU, Stanford's Director College, the John F. Kennedy School at Harvard, and the Director's College of the National Association of Corporate Directors, and has an Economics degree from Duke University. Phil was the CED 1997 Entrepreneur of the year. He is currently an Entrepreneurial Fellow at Wake Forest University. Phil may be reached at Johnston Tobin, LLC., 336-889-2900 or at Pjohnston@johnstontobin.com

ABOUT THE AUTHOR

Phil Johnston is Chairman and Chief Financial Officer of GET Interactive, Inc., a technology-based media company. He founded the Corporate Governance Practice Group with Nexsen Pruet PLLC, where he was Special Counsel for 2 years. In industry for 40 years, he is a "serial CEO" having been the head of 10 successful venture-backed companies in diverse, mostly technology industries - from piano manufacturing to microelectronics to biotechnology - earning him the CED Entrepreneur of the Year award in 1997. He has served as a director of five public companies including 14 years as a director of a NYSE listed company and numerous private companies. Even before the Enron, WorldCom era, he has been an advocate of continuing education as a requirement for board membership. He was an early advocate of director accountability. Putting this into practice, he completed Stanford Director College and National Association of Corporate Director (NACD) schools. His privileged academic background as an economics major at Duke University, (where he graduated after only three years and 48th in his class), The Stern Graduate School of Business at NYU, J.D. from the University of North Carolina Law School, and as a JFK School of Government scholar provide him platforms to communicate and guide the expectant entrepreneur and corporate director. More importantly, turning the crank as CEO of 2 public companies and living in the trenches of corporate board rooms for 40 full years gives Phil Johnston a true boots-on-the-ground perspective.

Phil's blog address is http://www. Web2ohTV.com.

Printed in the United States
96564LV00003B/232-234/A